February 2003

Dianna —
    You are a
wonderful blessing and
encouragement in your new
position in MOPs.
    May Jesus bless you
each step of the way as you
bless moms!
    And may your legacy
be bright and lasting ♡!
                    Deena Wilson

Presented to

_____

_____

                                    date

    from

A Mom's Legacy

*Five simple ways
to say yes to what
counts forever*

DEENA LEE WILSON

Regal

A Division of Gospel Light
Ventura, California, U.S.A.

Published by Regal Books
A Division of Gospel Light
Ventura, California, U.S.A.
Printed in U.S.A.

Regal Books is a ministry of Gospel Light, an evangelical Christian publisher
dedicated to serving the local church. We believe God's vision for Gospel Light is
to provide church leaders with biblical, user-friendly materials that will help them
evangelize, disciple and minister to children, youth and families.

It is our prayer that this Regal book will help you discover biblical truth for your
own life and help you meet the needs of others. May God richly bless you.

*For a free catalog of resources from Regal Books/Gospel Light please call your Christian
supplier or contact us at* 1-800-4-GOSPEL.

Cover Design by Kevin Keller
Interior Design by Rob Williams
Edited by Deena Davis

LIBRARY OF CONGRESS CATALOGING-IN-PUBLICATION DATA
　　　Wilson, Deena Lee, 1955-
　　　　A mom's legacy / by Deena Lee Wilson.
　　　　　　p.　　cm.
　　　Includes bibliographical references (p.　　　　　　　).
　　　ISBN 0-8307-2386-2 (hc.)
　　　1. Mothers—Religious life.　2. Motherhood—Religious aspects—Christianity.
　　　3. Wilson, Deena Lee, 1955-　　　　.　　　　I. Title.
　　　BV4529.18.W55　　1999
　　　248.8'431—dc21

99-37843
CIP

1 2 3 4 5 6 7 8 9 10 11 12 13 14 15 / 05 04 03 02 01 00 99

Rights for publishing this book in other languages are contracted by Gospel Literature
International (GLINT). GLINT also provides technical help for the adaptation,
translation and publishing of Bible study resources and books in scores of languages
worldwide. For further information, contact GLINT, P.O. Box 4060, Ontario, CA
91761-1003, U.S.A. You may also send E-mail to Glintint@aol.com, or visit their website
at www.glint.org.

For Alex,
my love,
and Chandler and Ethan,
my legacy.

For Mom,
who taught me to cherish beauty,
and Dad,
whose love for books, learning and
discovery I share.

And for all
who tenderly hold
little hands.

Contents

❧

Part One
Choosing to Invest in What Lasts

Your "Things Imperishable" Account

Part Two
Five Ways to Bring Lasting Hope
to Your Family

Bestowing Belonging and Identity
on Your Children

Celebrating Little Things and Small Beginnings

Deena Wilson is a woman I have had the privilege of knowing and loving since she made her first appearance at Aglow International offices in 1984.

This is the woman I want to introduce to you: Deena is a storyteller of unusual skill who will encourage you to see the everyday ways we can all leave a legacy of God's love from generation to generation. She will engage your heart in ways that will surprise you, just as she engaged my heart from the beginning.

I will never forget the first time I met this fresh-faced, lovely young woman. Not only was I drawn to her wonderful sense of humor, but also to a certain depth and sensitivity that was quietly apparent. She was close in age to my own daughter, and her vulnerability gave me the feeling that I wanted to take her under my wing, to walk with her, to be there for her in whatever small way I could.

When she moved to the Seattle area, Deena left behind her small-town Ohio roots and the close family she dearly loved. Her purpose was to begin a new season in her life by working at Aglow, but her journey was not without its cost. In those first few months, she experienced many lonely hours as a single woman before new friendships began to take root. Night after night as coworkers left the office to spend the evening with family, she went home to dinner at a table for one.

Then a handsome young man she knew from church became a friend. One day our family learned that Alex was invited to spend a week in Hawaii with some close friends of ours. When I realized that our family would be in Hawaii at the same time, we had the fun of "helping along" this budding relationship by including Deena in our vacation plans. Though a week in paradise didn't produce the results a "mother" would hope for, God was at work in each of their hearts. Months later, my husband and I were thrilled to see them at our door to show us the engagement ring!

As Deena continued her journey with her life partner, their future blossomed with possibilities. They were anxious to begin a family. Even as the months wore on without a sign, hope overcame discouragement. After two years, her hope swelled into joy as she felt new life inside her. But their rejoicing came to an abrupt end as they— we—walked through the wrenching loss of their long-awaited child, yet unborn. A year later, new life stirred again within Deena. Today they are patiently parenting two boys, who are bouncing with possibilities of their own.

Through the years, Deena, Alex and now their sons have been part of our extended family at summer picnics,

Christmas dinners and other gatherings. We have laughed, cried and shared with each other in ways that knit our hearts together with ties so tender, they could only be created by a master knitter.

Deena knits her stories like that, with tender ties that break your heart one minute and leave you bursting with laugher the next. Part of her writing gift comes rooted in the soil of legacy from Ohio. Every rich thing her parents put in her, God has developed and matured to shape the woman she has become.

She began this book out of her struggle to find meaning in the ordinary day-to-day-ness of motherhood. As Deena sought hard after God for the "why" in her often relentless routine, she discovered an eternal truth: Motherhood wasn't found in *maximizing* the moment but in *seeing eternity* in it. That truth aimed her at nurturing a destiny in God for two little boys and discovering a role in eternity for herself.

Jane Hansen
PRESIDENT
AGLOW INTERNATIONAL

Acknowledgments

My warm thank-yous go to:

My dear family, near and far, by birth and by choice—for your circle of love, one of my life's greatest treasures;

The following people at Regal Books: Bill Greig III and Kyle Duncan—for believing in me and in God's possibilities, even though my big block of writing time was the one hour when "Sesame Street" was on; Kim Bangs—for being a warm, encouraging voice at all the right moments; my editor, Deena Davis, for skillfully weeding and pruning my words;

My friend Darlene Kruezer; my mom, Ruth Duncan; and my oh-so-missed long-distance friend Elaine Keith—for faithfully praying our family through tendonitis, writer's block, chicken pox and computer glitches, and for calling this book into being on your knees;

Dana Shelford, Holli Gaines and Lois Larsen—for taking Chandler and Ethan under your wings with special TLC, trips to McDonalds, and play dates so I could write. I simply couldn't have done it without you;

Karen Anderson and Carol Greenwood—for listening and cheering me on;

My "Jewish moms" and friends, past and present, at

Aglow International headquarters—for drawing me into your hearts and lives;

Pastor Dan and Terry Hammer and my church family at Sonrise Chapel—for living the stories with us and loving us;

Linda Major—for praying as you made our house sparkle;

Alex, my husband—for setting roses beside the word processor and for being so supportive of my dream right through writer's angst, many meals out and an oft-distracted wife. Nothing can ever erase what your love has written in me.

Jesus, my Lord—for Your great faithfulness and for never, ever letting go of my hand. I'm sincerely Yours forever.

You Can Take It With You

It was almost time. Diane was waiting amidst all the taped-up boxes, her purse on her lap. This had caught her completely by surprise. In 30 or 40 years, yes. But she had never dreamed it would be so soon. Had she known, she might have gotten her hair done, written a few things down, cleared a few things up, worked a few things through. But here she was, and here was her family, gathered loosely around her, not too close. They were speaking in low tones. Occasionally someone wiped their eyes.

"Excuse me." She felt a gentle tap on her shoulder. "We're almost ready." The man was wearing bib overalls and a purple T-shirt and seemed to be in charge of the other workers. His voice was pleasant, almost musical.

Diane was on her feet right away, ready to direct the loading. Apparently, those were her things in the boxes. At least that was her understanding. So this must be like a company move. In a way, that was nice. She and her husband had moved four times. Each time the packing had been a nightmare. It was a relief to have someone else do all that.

"Just a minute more," the man said, suddenly at her elbow again.

She gestured toward the stacks of boxes. "All these things go, I guess." She pointed to a large box that looked ready to split its seams. "I hope the tape on that one holds."

He looked at her for a long moment, his eyes gentle. "You don't know then...no one has ever told you?"

"Told me what?"

"You can't take your boxes," he said quietly. "None of these come. Just you."

"But...but..." She pulled the strap of her purse up over her shoulder in a nervous gesture. She didn't have a clue what to say.

"We're leaving!" a voice called cheerfully from another corner of the room.

She felt a little rush of warm air, like a door swinging open and shut. But when she turned, she saw only another wall of her boxes.

"Will you please tell me what's going on?" she demanded of the purple-shirted man. "This just isn't exactly what I expected."

The man turned to her with a smile. "My coworkers have left. They won't be long. They're just going to go check on your investments. And hers."

Hers? Diane didn't know why she hadn't noticed the other lady in the room until now. The woman looked about the same age, and she was sitting on a wooden box, like a simple hope chest, with a strip of bright yellow strapping tape wrapped around it. That was all she appeared to have—that one box doubling for a chair. It was good that she didn't have more, because there wouldn't have been any room for the people mingling around her.

Diane wanted to call over to the lady, ask her if she had any idea what was going on here. But it looked like such a Hallmark moment with that little boy pressed close to her knee, and the conversation and quiet laughter of all the others. What was that lady doing, hostessing some sort of party or celebration? This hardly seemed to be the time. Well, she didn't want to intrude.

She turned back to the purple-shirted man. "You said your partners are checking on my investments? But they don't have my account numbers. They don't even know where I bank."

"That's true," he agreed with a smile. "But they have what they need to get into your T. I. account."

Was it too warm in this room? She needed a Diet Coke or something. Things were getting murkier by the minute.

"It's simpler than it seems at first," offered the man. "Your T. I. account is your Things Imperishable account. It's amazing, but everything that really lasts shows up in there—every loving word, every act of kindness, every hopeful deed you've ever done. Everything. Right down to hugging a little kid or giving someone a drink of cold water."

He paused and looked at her closely before going on. "You see, everything you put in your T. I. account is like a seed. It keeps compounding, keeps on growing. It's a long-term investment, but for those who are patient, the return is heavenly. It's not the whole picture, but the T. I. investments go a very long way toward helping people and families, cultures and nations find hope and grow strong. Few people realize that."

Diane stared at him. Who in the world was this guy anyway? She didn't know a thing about these T. I. accounts. She didn't know much about nations or cultures changing. But she did know some things about family and friends, and suddenly it seemed she could hardly see hers. They were standing back so far they were nearly hidden by all her boxes. Couldn't they come closer, gather around her? She had always wanted that; she could see that now. But life was so full, so busy. There was just never enough time.

Suddenly the purple-shirted man straightened, his eyes bright. "Listen!" he ordered. "It's them, bringing back her T. I. report."

From a long way off, Diane could hear muffled sounds and faraway excited shouting. At first she could barely make it out, but then it came closer, grew clearer. It sounded something like, "She's going! She's going!"

At that very moment, as if on cue, the other lady, the party-giving one, stood up eagerly, a radiant smile on her face.

Diane bent forward, straining at the sounds. Why, she wondered, did it suddenly seem like the most important thing in the world to not miss this—that she hear the words clearly? The shouts were drawing even closer now, a melodious chorus of voices. What was it they were saying? Suddenly, Diane's eyes widened. No, they weren't shouting, "She's going! She's going!" The words were "They're growing! They're growing!" The sounds grew richer, more resonant as they drew near. Now the voices were all beginning to flow together, like rivers of music.

All at once there was the rush of warm air again, like an opening door. The music swirled into the room, ribboning its bright way around the boxes, the party lady and her visitors and around Diane. It filled the room like a cathedral chorus. It was the most glorious sound she had ever heard.

Diane looked up at the purple-shirted man. He looked radiant, lit up from the inside. He bent down close to Diane's ear. "You see," he said, "there are thousands of seeds of love she has planted in other hearts and they are still growing. Heaven is rejoicing over every single one. This is her benediction music. And that," he pointed to the box the woman had been sitting on, "is the box she gets to take with her." Diane turned to see two workers in overalls bending down to carefully lift the wooden chest.

"Now, wait a minute," Diane protested, "That's not fair. I thought you said no boxes were allowed. I thought you said I can't take any of my stuff with me."

"That's right," said the purple-shirted man. "Stuff never comes. All anyone ever gets to bring with them is their benediction music—and this one box. Look at the label when it comes past us."

Well, I most certainly will! Diane thought. She was dying to know. As the music soared and the workers passed her, cradling the box like it was some sort of national treasure, Diane tipped her head to read the label. There on the yellow tape, in big red letters, was printed just one word: "Relationships."

"You know, that is all you ever really keep," she could hear the purple-shirted man saying behind her. "All you keep...keep...keep."

Why was he repeating that word? Did he think she couldn't hear him? "Keep. Keep. Keep. Beep. Beep. Beep."

Diane rolled over with a groan and punched off her alarm. The cat was nosing her elbow as weak morning sun filtered through the blinds. She could hear thumps and giggles through the wall and knew the kids were awake. She rubbed her eyes and tried to remember what day it was. Then she just lay there for a minute on her back, thinking, looking straight up at the ceiling.

Part One

Choosing to Invest in What Lasts

Every mother is like Moses.
She does not enter the Promised Land.
She prepares a world she will not see.[1]

POPE PAUL VI

Life is too short to be small.[2]

BENJAMIN DISRAELI

Leaving an Empty Dish, or Planting Shade Trees?

*I*T WAS THE BUSINESS ABOUT THE CHEESE-BALL THAT GOT TO ME. I NEVER EVEN USED TO READ THE OBITUARIES, BUT FOR SOME reason I do now. Not every day, but frequently. I go through the newspaper in a certain order: I start with the headline and front page so I know what new crisis I'm supposed to worry about. I read the comics last so I remember to keep it all in perspective. Somewhere in between I scan the obituaries.

It isn't as if I expect to see my former piano teacher listed, or someone my dad worked with, or the bus driver who was on my daily route to college. And that's not only because I've never played the piano or gone to college, but because I'm not originally from the Pacific Northwest. My roots are in the Midwest — Columbus, Ohio, to be exact. So when I read the obituaries in Seattle, I'm not really expecting to see a name I recognize.

I guess I read the obituaries because it fascinates me that a life can be condensed into a little rectangle of newsprint no larger than a carefully folded tissue. Of course, it can't be. Not really. But reading an obituary is like looking at a framed miniature portrait. You see at a glance the person's name (even that dreaded middle name they kept a secret), where he or she was born, the person's life's work, how many children they had, where the family eventually called home, whether a life of faith held meaning for the deceased. In an obituary—although the picture may be a little grainy and out of focus—you see something of legacy. You see something of what remains when everything is said and done: Martin Miller, architect and WWII veteran. Jamie Wise, our little lamb. Big sister to Ryan. Rita Riazo, everyone's mom. Wonderful listener and friend.

One day I was scanning the obituaries when I came to one that made my jaw drop. I don't remember this dear lady's name, and I wouldn't think of using it anyway. But her obituary was a straightforward "just the facts, ma'am" report. As I remember, there was little, if any, mention of what she had enjoyed or valued or achieved. The one dubious personal touch was this admission: "She made a great cheeseball."

I backed up and read it again. Unfortunately, it still said the same thing. She made a great cheeseball. That's it. *Please,* I thought, *somebody tell me that a stressed-out copywriter with a migraine, a deadline and very few details put this together.* I am positive this woman's crowning glory in life was *not* a nut-studded ball with a perfect little cherry on top. But that is pretty much all the obituary said. No, that's not accurate. There was one closing note just before the name of the funeral home and when the service would be held: "At the reception, her cousin will be serving a cheeseball in her honor."

I am not making this up, and I'm certainly not trying to be disrespectful. But I must have been nearly hyperventilating as my mind flashed ahead to my own final days. I imagined the phone ringing at the home of my writer friend, Carol, who is an enviable wonder with words. She can make them sing. I visualized our imaginary conversation going something like this:

"Carol, when I die, would you please write something touching for my obituary? Something with more dignity and substance to it than a cheeseball kind of thing?"

I imagined a long, questioning silence at the other end of the line. Then she replied in her usual steadying way, "Umm...sure. Yes. All right. Deena...is everything okay? Getting out much?"

No kidding, I would absolutely turn over in my grave if an unknown someone wrote my obituary and came up with something even close to "Deena's spice rack was always so perfectly alphabetized" or "Her cat was devoted to her" or "She ran her Eureka like a pro." That is why I need to have a talk with Carol. It's only fair that I give her some advance notice, so she can think through a few meaningful phrases—a handful of praiseworthy things to say about me—and have a definite game plan when my time comes.

I don't want her clicking her pen against her teeth, staring at the blank sheet of paper and musing, "Deena...

Deena. Now, what is there to say about her?" And if Carol's day comes before mine, I'll just have to think this whole thing through again.

What gives me a chill down to my toes is the thought that it might actually be possible for me to live a life about which few noteworthy things could be said. It makes me swallow hard.

It isn't a meaningless life I fear, and that's because of a few things I believe to be impossible. For instance, it is impossible for a toddler to remain nonsticky for more than an hour unless he or she is unconscious (and maybe not even then). It is impossible for cats to act servile and dependent and owned, as if they were possessions of the people who feed them, brush them and pay all their vet bills. It is impossible for anyone, anywhere, anytime to live a life that doesn't matter. Life matters. Always.

God, the One who sees everything, treasures my life and yours. He treasures every life He has created. We may live foolishly, but we can never live invisibly. He watches. He loves us.

We may live blindly and ungratefully; we may live below every hope God has in His heart for us. Yet, something from above is inescapably with us and within us—God's image. We may try to deface it, erase it, replace it, but still He shows through. Where life is, God is. Where God is, there is meaning. So I can never live a worthless life, and neither can anyone else. But a squandered life? A small life? An "empty dish" life? That's another matter.

Dale Turner, a columnist in the *Seattle Times*, made this observation:

Two very important days in every life are the day we are born and the day we know why we were born. There are many people, living and dead, who never experienced that second day. It is as Isaac Watts once wrote:

> *Most people creep into the world*
> *And know no reason why they are born.*
> *Except to consume the corn and fish*
> *And leave behind...an empty dish.*[3]

I know your mom probably told you the same thing my mom told me — clean your plate; but this kind of empty dish isn't exactly what our moms had in mind. If all my friend Carol, or anyone else, can remember about me when I'm gone is that I was a wife and mom, that I loved popcorn and hated brussels sprouts, that I had perpetually cold feet, that I could get lost getting towels out of my linen closet, then my "dish" on my day of departure will be woefully empty.

When all is said and done, my legacy will be that I was a consumer of goods and services, of time and treasure, of opportunities and other people. Maybe I ate well, enjoyed my life (sort of), loosened my belt and cleaned my plate. But that would be about it. The sad reality would be that I was born but never really understood why.

An empty dish legacy just doesn't do it for me. I've known for a long time that I'm designed for something more than that.

❦ ❦ ❦

One day God gave me a living illustration of what that "something more" might be about, weighing in at about seven or eight pounds of wonder and wetness.

I'm not sure, but there may have been a moment when God nodded, flexed His creative fingers and said with a knowing smile, "Yes, it is time. Let us send her a baby made in her and Alex's image. This babe will be blissfully unaware that I, the Lord, divided day from night an eternity ago. He will cheweth like a beaver along the freshly painted banister. He will quickly sprout into a toddler. He will screech like a tropical bird as he gallops through the house. He will playfully toss his rubber boots onto a hot burner. He will wind his way around and under every clothing rack in the mall and wind his mom's heart around his finger.

"On his way to utterly exhausting her, he will energize and engage her in a way she never dreamed possible. Like her waistline, her soul will be incredibly stretched, never to return to its former size. Yea, it will be only in the three quiet minutes she has in the next five years that she will begin to realize that a miracle has happened: This child has truly helped set her heart free from itself. And she has lived to tell it."

Well, it might have gone something like that. I don't know. But five years into motherhood, I do know this: It was a very wise someone who suggested that choosing to have a child is choosing to have your heart walk around outside your body for the rest of your life. When I look at my two sons, five-year-old Chandler and almost-three Ethan, it seems a very good—though occasionally perilous—place for my heart to be. Outside myself.

Speaking of outside, let me pursue a little bunny trail and say that my husband, Alex, loves the outdoors. For a time he even considered a career in forestry. Though I am beginning to warm up to things wild, I usually am more drawn to things written. I enjoy a nest with four walls, carpeting, indoor plumbing and a good reading light.

Last Christmas Alex and I bought each other shirts with wording emblazoned across the fronts. His shirt, appropriately forest green with clean white lettering, exhorts, "Go outside." My shirt protests, "So many books...so little time."

When we face each other wearing our shirts, we can carry on a brief conversation without having to say a single word. This can save us a lot of time, which is always a plus when you have young children. This aside briefly introduces you to my husband (the man with a collapsible rake in his hand and pine needles on his very nice broad shoulders).

But let me return to my point that God has used parenting to draw my heart outside myself in ways I would never have imagined. Here is a picturesque, outdoorsy example of where that exodus has been bringing me. Next to learning to love God more, I want to spend my life planting shade trees. Now hold on. I know this might seem like an odd aspiration for someone who is not exactly a nature girl and who is doing well to distinguish between a begonia and a bonsai. But I'm speaking figuratively, not literally. Let me explain myself with the help of Elton Trueblood.

> A man has made at least a start on discovering the meaning of human life when he plants shade trees under which he knows full well he will never sit.[4]

Mr. Trueblood isn't, of course, talking about root balls and sharp spades, saplings and soil. He's talking about digging down deep and seeing far. He is talking about a life more invested in giving than getting, an other-centered, forward-looking life. He is talking about spreading some heaven-sent cooling shade and shelter that will last for a very long time. That's the stuff of legacy. I think Mr. Trueblood would get along famously with William James, who penned, "The greatest use of life is to spend it for something that will outlast it."[5]

❀ ❀ ❀

"Eeeeeeethan!" I lunged to rescue a paper from my desk. Too late. Little Ethan had been contentedly practicing his cutting as I keyboarded away on this book.

Snip, snip. It was companionable. It was cute. Until those blunt purple scissors, awkwardly looped on toddler fingers, acquired a taste for bigger and better things than scrap paper.

The *Jaws* theme song should have been playing as the scissors targeted their next unsuspecting victim—the acceptance letter from my publisher, saying yes to this, my first book. Yes to my lifelong dream. Yes to all sorts of bright possibilities. That hallmark letter, a shining bit of personal history, had been destined for a nice frame and a spot on our study wall. Until—*augggh!*—it was gashed by the Great Snipper.

It took a few minutes. It took a few tears. Later on, it might take a little tape. But as I sat there in my bathrobe, staring mournfully at my wounded letter and my wide-eyed little one, something began to dawn on me. This book is all about my longing to live and love well, to make a difference, to celebrate what counts and what lasts in a "hurry-up" world. To learn to say yes to God and to life.

My letter may last 20 or even 50 years before it yellows and crumbles. Paper wasn't made to last. But Ethan? He was made to last. You and I were created to last. That's easy to forget, isn't it? Usually the eternal value of other people is not exactly uppermost in my mind. I need to be nudged, especially at those times when my highest aspiration is simply to find my way out of the jungle of the day. Maybe you can relate.

❦ ❦ ❦

One evening, as an antidote to an especially stressful week, Alex pulled out a puzzle and we settled in front of the fireplace for some interlocking entertainment. Now this is great, I thought. Cheap, creative, satisfying.

The puzzle was a tranquil country scene, dissected into little pieces—500 of them. About 450 pieces were parts of bushes and trees, all in muted shades of green and brown. After about a half hour of "relaxing," I had connected five pieces. My back and neck muscles were twisted as tight as a wrung washcloth; my eyes were bloodshot and I was ready to scream like a hyena.

"How are you doing?" Alex hummed as he popped another piece into place. He appeared to be the epitome of calm and leisure.

"Fine," I snapped. "I'm just fine." I had the strongest urge to hurl myself or the puzzle against the nearest wall and end the misery. A puzzle is supposed to be therapeutic, but let me tell you, a hot tub it ain't.

The way the marvels of modern life can leave us fragmented, I don't think many of us are searching for something more to do or to fit together. Few of us need 500 or so extra pieces to fill out our days. That's one reason I've tried to keep this book mercifully simple.

It's been said that a book is a garden you can hold in your hand. So let me offer you a handful of ideas: five—not 500—opportunities to live for what matters and what lasts. I'd like to suggest five ways to spread some restorative shade and hope to those you love: *share your stories, treasure little things, live in the now, keep a room of your own* and *remember heaven.*

I invite you into this season of life at our house and, just for fun, I'll tell you a few stories. As Michael E. Williams has said, it is stories that "transform sojourners into kinfolk and strangers into friends."[6] That sounds good to me.

I don't know what season of life you may be in, but no matter what your age, if you're warm and breathing, you are already leaving your legacy. Honestly. Legacy leaving doesn't mysteriously kick in when you begin to carry the number of your hair-color formula in your wallet, or when you suddenly notice that all professionals appear to be roughly 16 years old, or when by some strange compulsion you begin to fold and save used wrapping paper exactly like your mother does. Oh, no.

Like the electricity meters at our homes, legacy living runs continuously, sometimes slowly, sometimes alarmingly fast.

Legacy living and leaving goes on all the time, from our first until our final day, from dawn to sunset. Just like the electricity meters at our homes, legacy living runs continuously: sometimes slowly, sometimes alarmingly fast.

A story begs to be told here—the one about a promised trip to the zoo with my son Chandler. He was four, and he was wrestling with the unwelcome concept that not all things promised happen right now. No matter that he was still in his jammies, that Mommy was still without makeup, that the day's to-do list stretched far beyond the day's to-do hours. With a preschooler's sense of immediacy, he was ready to click his heels and magically be on location at the zoo, sliding on the lion statues and mimicking the monkeys.

"Honey, we're going to the zoo tomorrow, " I explained for the third time.

Chandler sighed and frowned. I could see his mental wheels spinning. Tomorrow might mean a long, long time from now, or at the worst, it might mean never.

I swiped the kitchen table with the dishcloth, held up one finger and gave him the gift of context. "Tomorrow. That's one more sleep, punkin'. I promise."

The next morning as he crunched his cereal, I made the grand announcement. "Chandy, we're going to the zoo today."

He was stunned, half-dubious. "Today?!"

I nodded and smiled. "Today. As soon as we get dressed."

He pondered this thunderbolt for a moment. Then his expression brightened and he laughed triumphantly as if he'd just gotten the punch line of a joke. "Ohhh... I get it! Today is tomorrow!"

Yes. That's just it. Today is indeed tomorrow, in so many ways. How we live today molds the tomorrow we will find in our hands. As Annie Dillard has said, "How we spend our days is, of course, how we spend our lives."[7]

Now I just need to live remembering that. It will go a long way toward having something worthwhile to leave.

❧ ❧ ❧

I'm not planning on taking flight anytime soon, but the reality is that I don't have any guarantees on my next breath or my next heartbeat. Each one is a pure gift. But as long as I find myself here in this moment and still in my skin, I still have time on the clock. My stay in this life isn't finished yet. So it makes sense to me to go ahead and do now whatever it is I feel I am here to do.

When I read Ephesians 2:10, it's always good news for me. "For we are God's workmanship, created in Christ Jesus to do good works, which God prepared in advance for us to do." Here's my up-close-and-personal version: God has created me to make a lasting difference in my world, to touch lives with a legacy that only I can plant and only He can grow. Here I am—a woman, a wife, a daughter, a mom finding bathrooms and buckling car seats—on the brink of a brand-new millennium. I am not here by accident or coincidence. I'm here by God's design, for His reasons. So how do I want to live, and what do I want to leave?

I only need to think about it if I want some choice in the whole matter. I already have the gift of a significant life whether I want it or not. I can no more change that than I can make the sky orange. Just like you, I simply can't help it; God has seen to that. But if I want a "shade tree" life — a life lived on purpose that moves and matters for good — it's going to take some doing. If I want a giving, touchable, invitational life that points joyfully to God and to things that last, I will have to make some choices. It will take some thought and some prayer. It will take some intention and some invention. Some two-part harmony between me and God. Some swimming upstream in a downstream current.

"Few...have cared enough to defy [these] hurried values," Tim Hansel says. "Fewer still have the detachment, the courage and commitment to establish themselves in the timeless priorities that I am finding in the Scriptures, to risk the consequences of a lifestyle that is deliberately chosen rather than just accepted."[8] You see, a life-giving legacy doesn't happen automatically or by osmosis, any more than a shade tree scopes out a good spot in the yard, thumps across the lawn on its root ball, scrapes out a hole and plants itself. I don't think so. Planting is up to us.

❦ ❦ ❦

When I leave life, I hope the angels will not be bumping wing tips as they cluster around me whispering, "Yes, yes, she's going...."

I have a different scenario in mind, provided it's OK with the Lord, of course. Naturally I want my loved ones circled around me to pray, to remember, to laugh, to touch, to help me finish...and begin. But the best benediction of all would be this: I'd love for the angels to make their rounds and do a progress check on every seedling of hope, every sapling of truth or joy, every bit of God in me that I ever planted in someone else's heart. Then the last thing I would be hearing as I left would be a shouted chorus of angelic reports, echoing all the way to heaven: "They're growing! They're growing!" Not just "She's going," but "They're growing!" Now that's what I'd call an exquisite exit.

I'll be the first to admit that it isn't easy or comfortable to think about my own exit, especially as I seem to be at the entrance, the beginning of so much. At our house we're still doing diapers and doggies and dot-to-dot. But this is also the perfect time to begin planting a legacy. The surprising thing is that opportunities crop up at the most unexpected times.

A few weeks ago, five-year-old Chandler and I sat in our van. (Have you heard the one about the mom who said she never dreamed she'd spend one night delivering in the hospital and 16 years delivering in the van?) Anyway, we had just pulled into our driveway. I reached to snap off the ignition and suddenly found 48 pounds of boy in my lap.

He was an octopus child, with eight arms simultaneously extended to discover what all those usually forbidden levers, lights and buttons around the dashboard are for.

Just when I was feeling like a glorified seat cushion and was ready to climb out, Chandler started talking about kings. Where this topic came from I'll never know, but it did come and we ended up going everywhere with it. There was David and Saul, we remembered, and Josiah, the boy king (or was that Joash?). There were brave and bad kings, so-so and awesome kings. Chandler, who was born ready to take charge, sat enthroned on my lap, delightedly commanding the wipers to swish and the headlights to flash. And all the while, he kept talking kings.

"What does a good king, a really good leader do, Chandy?" I asked him.

"I'm not sure," he replied, while walking his fingers all round the steering wheel. We had talked about this before, a couple of times. Now, accompanied by his occasional honk on the horn, I decided to tell him again, to plant again.

"Well, the best leader helps his people." I was talking into the curls at the crown of his perfect head, my getting-too-big-for-my-lap son. "The way he helps them most is by showing them how to love God." Someday, perhaps even in a someday I won't see, Chandler is going to lead. I know this the way women sometimes do.

"Sunshine, do you know what is the very most important thing of all?" I asked.

He must have heard the sudden urgency in my voice, which surprised us both. How had we leapfrogged from discussing high and low headlight beams to good and bad kings to life's brightest purpose? Chandler twisted around to look at me, waiting, his questioning eyes as deep as windows into other worlds.

"Love Jesus forever," I said. Three simple words. So-small words. Change-everything words. Just like "I love you" or "It is finished" or "Always come home." Words to return to in a life with as many twists and turns as our in-the-van chat. Words to shade and shelter one small boy from the precariousness of one big world. *Love Jesus forever.*

"Okay," Chandler said quietly. He turned around and sat motionless, looking straight ahead. I wondered if he was trying to absorb the significance of this tender moment.

"Mommy?" He turned his face up toward mine again, like a flower.

"Uh-huh?" I was poised and ready.

"Look!" he hooted, jabbing with his finger. "There sure is a lot of bird poop on our window!"

Well, it could have been worse. He could have been sitting there calculating that he only has 3,750 days before he can get his driver's license.

Counting days is not such a bad idea. But making your days count is even better. That, certainly, is what living and leaving a legacy is all about.

Because I Love a Good Story...

I had this dream that I died and went to heaven. I was 20 minutes late. I suddenly realized I was wearing one earring, no lipstick and the blouse with the big catsup stain down the front.

"I see that you're the mom of small children," Saint Peter said with a kind smile. He bent to consult his book. "And you've sent up a number of special requests."

I was awed and delighted. "Somebody actually wrote them down?"

"Oh, yes," he replied. "Let's just review these to make sure you have no changes. You've asked for a self-cleaning kitchen floor that no longer gets so sticky it pulls off your slippers?"

"Why, that's right!" I said, surprised and pleased.

"And a robe without little silver nose trails all around the bottom half...and a purse with more real lady things like perfume, and fewer petrified animal crackers and tubes of diaper-rash cream?"

I was impressed. "Whoever took those notes was very thorough," I said.

"We aim to please. Let's see...about talks with your four-year-old son. You've requested that certain discussions be limited to five minutes or less. Talks about things such as whether it's good to wash your feet in apple juice, or questions about why God doesn't give a boy a lizard tongue if he has really, really prayed for one."

My head bobbed up and down enthusiastically.

Saint Pete made a check mark. "And you'd like whoever came up with the idea of those itty, bitty Lego pieces to be publicly executed?"

My face reddened. "Well, at least flogged. Right alongside whoever dreamed up the phrase, 'This toy will entertain your child for hours'."

Saint Pete lowered his head and gave me a long, searching look over the top of his rose-colored glasses. "We'll see what we can do," he murmured.

I was beginning to feel confident that heaven was truly going to be a heavenly place. I leaned on the desk. "Pete, you want to know what really entertains a child for hours? Let me tell you. Stuffing things into other things; it doesn't matter what. Wedge your baby brother under the couch. Shove a pea up your nose. Cram a half-eaten apple into the vacuum cleaner hose. Believe me, I know."

Saint Pete squinted slightly and massaged his temple with one hand. "Now, you asked to be able to shave both legs without being interrupted?"

"Yes, yes! Unless there's a true emergency. I mean something more life-threatening than the popsicle truck driving by."

By now a line of people was forming behind me. "You'd like an ice cream cone, a stick of gum, even a breath mint all to yourself?" Pete asked.

"Right!" My eyes glowed greedily. "Well...unless the kids were really in need of a little bite of something. They are both in a growth spurt right now."

Pete never missed a beat. "You'd like to never again have to plunge your hands into any unidentified substance."

"Absolutely! Then again, unless nobody else would clean it up and it would get tracked all over creation."

Pete pressed on. "You'd like no more days when the baby blows out his diaper, your preschooler runs to the living room with an indelible red marker, the cat throws up and the phone rings—all at the same time?"

"Hallelujah!" I crowed. "Well, at least fewer days like that."

"Uh-huh." He made a quick note. "And no more kids' song tapes playing for the millionth time, no one kicking the back of your seat in the van, no one repeating, 'I am a space alien—beep' over and over. Just peace and serenity. Forever."

"Forever?" I blinked and swallowed hard. "Forever

is a really long time, isn't it?"

Saint Peter clapped his big book shut and leaned across the desk, his white beard quivering. "Mrs. Wilson, it's quite clear to me what's going on here."

My eyes widened.

"Why, you don't belong here! You still have blocks to step on in the middle of the night. You still have noses to wipe, owies to kiss, slugs and sand to dump out of jeans pockets. I know you love poetry, so let me put this in the words of a poet: Mrs. Wilson, you still have promises to keep and miles of peanut butter sandwiches to make before you sleep!"

I pulled out a wet wipe and dabbed at my eyes. "Okay...okay! It's just that I trained for a mothering sprint and then found out it's a marathon!"

Pete reached out and gently touched my arm.

"I guess," I snuffled, "I guess I just need an oasis, not an eternity."

"Trust the Lord," Pete said softly. "Nobody does a better oasis than He does."

I nodded and looked at him through reddened eyes. "You're going to send me back down there, aren't you? But before you do, can I ask you for one eeny, beeny favor?"

I looked furtively both ways, then slipped him a big jar of homemade applesauce. "Could you 'accidentally' set me down in Maui? Pleeeease?!!"

Part Two

Five Ways to
Bring Lasting Hope
to Your Family

*Tell it to your children,
and let your children tell it
to their children, and their children
to the next generation.*

JOEL 1:3

❧

*The real histories of families
aren't the records
of births, deaths, and marriages.
They are the stories
told after dessert,
when the coffee's been served and
everyone's too full to move.* [1]

FREDERICK WATERMAN

Chapter Two

Share Your
Stories

E KNOW QUITE A BIT ABOUT BAGS AT OUR HOUSE. THERE IS THE EVER-PRESENT DIAPER BAG, WHICH I AM CONVINCED THEY surgically stapled to my shoulder sometime during Chandler's delivery. There are plastic grocery bags that multiply like rabbits on our darkened garage shelf and also make pretty decent Superman capes if you poke your arms backward through the carrying holes. Then there are the occasional under-the-eye "When was the last time I slept?" bags, which beg for immediate photo retouching or concealer bought in bulk, although the eye bags are becoming less frequent as our boys grow.

With some help, I've identified an entirely different kind of bag that I think I've instinctively known about since childhood. I can't begin to count the times in my life I've said to someone, "Oh, remember when...?" or "Have I ever told you about...?" Now I know I was reaching down into my "story bag."

A story bag is what writer Alida Gertsie has named the place inside us where a lifetime of memories live. She suggests that everyone carries a story bag in their hearts, whether they open it many times a day or keep the drawstring pulled tightly shut.[2] Inside my story bag is a treasure of untold worth—the lessons and longings, the experiences and stories of my lifetime.

It doesn't take much to trigger a flood of remembrances

in me. I was a sensitive preschooler, adoring my big brother completely and without apology, and weeping brokenheartedly when the "skins" got peeled off my bright new crayons.

I was a little girl with an imagination bigger than I was, who single-handedly wrote and illustrated *Frog Life* magazine (circulation: one) for my stuffed frog and was positive that kids never, ever breathe while sleeping.

I was a searching, studious teenager, dragging a stiff leather book satchel that scraped fine red lines on the side of my legs. I was an eager graduate looking for my place in the world while exploring Roman ruins...sinking my teeth into a real Italian pizza in Naples...naively concluding that a bidet was a clever contraption for soaking weary feet.

A few years passed and I was a 20-something pilgrim, standing in knee-high grass by the Sea of Galilee, imagining the crowds that thronged to hear Jesus. I went home forever changed.

I was a Midwestern girl, whispering to God, "Please push me," as I walked with knocking knees into the belly of a plane bound for Seattle and a new life. Me. The wife who has loved her husband, rocked her babies, and lived a lot of ordinary days. The woman and dreamer and little girl all rolled into one, twirling in her dad's arms to "In the Mood" at his 50th wedding anniversary. Looking back at these life snapshots, I agree with the wise someone who noted that the nice part about getting older is that you get to keep all the ages you've already been.

Of course, I'm not the first person to feel deeply or to travel, to move to new lands or marry, and I certainly won't be the last. But as writer Anne Lamott notes, "All of us can sing the same song, and there will still be four billion different renditions."[3] In other words, everyone is living a life, but nobody else is living my life. And that is why no one else can tell my stories (or yours).

Nobody else was ever nicknamed "Miss Mouse" by my father. No one else will ever be my parents' third child, my sister's "favorite"—and only—sister, the wife who celebrated with Alex over our wonderful first home with the hideous avocado tile, or the mom who heard my son Ethan's first prayer. Those treasures are mine to keep. And, of course, they are mine to share with you if I want to dip into my story bag and pull out an everyday or an extraordinary story—something I've observed, something I've learned or experienced, someone I've met or someone I've become.

෯ ෯ ෯

It seems to be somehow that my own life isn't all that shines when I share a story and pass along a small gift of myself. A song I love, "The Story Goes On" celebrates that our shared experiences, big or small, profound or funny, can help someone else through the dark "'cause His love finds its way into the night through the pages of our lives."[4]

I felt like someone was reading the pages of my life in the grocery store the other day. I was bent over the refrigerator case, checking out the beef. Out of the corner of my eye, I saw a fellow shopper jabbing the shrink-wrapped packages so hard I was sure she would poke a hole right through the plastic.

She shot me a look of dismay. "Man! Six dollars a pound for that steak! I don't think so!"

"It's high, isn't it?" I commiserated.

She poked on. "I'm beat. Just doing the best I can." I could smell the heavy odor of cigarettes as she sighed and shook her head. "I want to do like my momma would want."

Before I knew it, I was murmuring, "I'm so sorry," as she told me about her mom's recent illness and death, her sisters too busy to help, her missionary brother too far away to come and her own blind, painful wrestle with a loss too deep to understand. I listened, remembering the times when I have said my own unthinkable good-byes. So different from what she was describing. So very much the same.

I said something like, "God is close." I didn't want to offer a cliché—some sort of "feel good" Band-Aid—when her world was off its axis. "When we hurt, God is with us.

He will help you." I said this, what I had so needed to hear myself when finality closed the door on me, and my life was forever changed. It wasn't my mom I'd lost. It was my baby, a dream, my life and future as I had hoped for it to be.

"I talk to Momma every day," she said, tossing a package of meat into her cart. "I do...I need to." She looked at me through dark eyes. "You go to church anywhere? I got a feeling you do."

I suddenly realized how little this conversation had to do with the price of beef and how much it had to do with two women and our stories—our unique yet common journeys of life and love and loss that intersected if only for a healing moment. Maybe something I said—something lifted from my story bag or even the person I am— helped to break her fall and bring her a new breath of courage. I hope so. That, I believe, is the promise of our stories, whether we are speaking them into a microphone at a crowded women's meeting or simply telling them in a quiet moment of shared sorrow and hope in a grocery store aisle.

◦◦◦

I don't need much to tell my stories. I don't know about you, but those Mother-Goose-style bonnets and little reading glasses don't do a thing for me. I can also forgo the rocking chair. I don't need to become a grandma or some sort of a Garrison Keillor to tell my stories; I can just be me. I can talk with you over my fence, by cell phone, behind a desk or across a café table. You can be my relative or a neighbor, a mom at the park or a fellow shopper in the return line at the mall.

If, in an appropriate moment, I mention the snap-dragons I grew this summer just to show my boys how to pinch the little jawlike blossoms and make them "talk," like I pinched them as a child, maybe you will see something of who I am, and feel invited in.

If I share sometime about that desperate morning I played musical beds with my nursing infant as he profusely burped up on every clean sheet in the house (after changing the sheets had been the one shining accomplishment the day before), maybe you'll laugh with recognition and feel a little less alone in your parenting. If I tell you about the man I watched coax a frightened toad out of the corner of an outside elevator (a gentle man who would later became my husband), maybe you will shake your head with me in wonder at God's mysterious appointments. Maybe you'll even tell me about some "appointments" of your own.

Maybe you and some of your stories will be medicine or music for me. Maybe they will rekindle hope for me in a twilight place and challenge me to blow the dust off an old dream, or offer me the tonic of laughter, infuse me with courage to make a long-awaited change or inspire me with tenacity to keep on trying. Some of your stories can be as simple as describing the white-knuckle experience of your teenager learning to drive, the perfect dress that makes you look a good 10 pounds thinner, the promising dinner you incinerated under the broiler last night. Those stories count, too.

I can't help but notice that people everywhere seem drawn to a good story as irresistibly as a late-night snacker is drawn to the refrigerator light. Although we have the world at the touch of a button, so to speak, it seems to me there is a whole universe inside us that our pentium processors, compact disc players and stereophonic televisions just can't touch. We need each other and we need our stories.

❦ ❦ ❦

A few weeks ago I slipped a shaggy lion puppet on my hand while playing nanny to a group of two-year-olds. Now keep in mind, this is the generation with a dizzying array of electronic toys in their toy boxes. These are kids who cut their teeth on a computer keyboard. Yet, in seconds I had five or six toddlers Velcroed to my ankles in wide-eyed anticipation of hearing that lion tell his tale.

Why is it that stories seem to hold their appeal at any

age? I know they somehow squeeze right past all my inhibitions and adult sophistication right into my heart.

Recently, Alex told me about a summer evening when he was a skinny 13-year-old, staring at a television screen as Neil Armstrong put that first pillowed foot into moondust. Later, Alex slipped into the cool backyard and trained the big, black family binoculars on the moon. It is an image so very like him—the boy he was, the man he would become, standing barefoot and earthbound in the moonlight, head lifted. Quietly observing, appreciating, wondering. It is a story that draws me close to him, one I can't forget.

෯ ෯ ෯

Isn't it something that when God decided to put out a book about Himself to draw us close to Him—a book for all people in all cultures, in every situation and for all time—He created a sacred Storybook? Why didn't Jesus come flashing a three-second image at us or speak in our average 13-second TV sound bite? Why didn't He bring some visuals with Him—offer a website, maybe, or at least a flipchart or diagram, pie graph or printout to help us understand God? Maybe it was because Jesus Himself was the visual, the image of God, a living story in progress. He came to us with straw in His hair, splinters in His fingers and a story bag in His heart.

For three years, Jesus spilled out His story bag in city squares and on country roads, in the hills and on beaches, for crowds of thousands and for an audience of one. He told of the collapsed tower in the daily headlines[5] and Father Abraham from ages past. He spoke of common people and kings, lilies and lambs, lost coins and golden opportunities, weeping fathers and wayward children, matchless pearls and meaningful life.

When Jesus told His stories, the businessman on his lunch break stopped chewing midbite; the tired mom with her baby on her hip felt new strength; the teenager with a boatload of anger blinked, twisted the edge of his robe and wondered. When Jesus spoke, there were no dry commands and lengthy theological statements about how God acted. There were magnetic, tell-it-again stories about who God was—God revelations. We, too, reveal ourselves in stories, if we want to.

I wanted to the other night as I sat with my back against the wall (literally). Chandler and Ethan were scrubbed, pajamaed and story ready as we sat on Chandler's bed. Rather than reaching for a Richard Scarry book or Veggie Tales or a Berenstain Bears book, I decided, with a little trepidation, to reach for me. Was there an age-appropriate tale from my own childhood I could tell them? Would their eyes glaze over? Would they suddenly decide to pursue something more entertaining like trying to fit both legs into one leg hole of their pajamas?

"No pictures this time," Chandler informed Ethan.

Ethan snuggled close anyway.

I came up with the tale of the bisected trike. The story line was pretty simple. When I was four or five, my beloved green tricycle, which had given me hours of riding enjoyment, met with a terrible fate. As I was cruising up and down the sidewalk one day, I suddenly made a hard stop and an even harder ejection landing. While I lay on the ground near the seat and back tires, I watched in astonishment as my handlebars and front wheel made a break for freedom. My tricycle had snapped in two. I was sure it was my fault.

As my story unfolded, it turned out that Chandler's comment about the pictures was only half right. True, there were no colorful pictures in a book to look at, but I could feel both boys reading my face. I told them about my confession to my mom and dad, and my relief that a flawed trike, not a flawed me, was to blame. And then came the happy ending. A few days later I watched my dad lift my repaired trike from the car trunk, and I ran my finger over the magic silver weld where the break had once been. I told the story as the simple childhood tale that it was. It took about three minutes, tops.

Then, partly because Chandler and Ethan were fairly non-squirmy and someone piped up, "Do another one!"and partly because I was beginning to enjoy myself, I meandered into a few more stories. There was the time I courted calamity by almost hosing down a wasps' nest while washing the front porch. The time my coal-black cat, Oreo, satisfied her sweet tooth and became a certified cat burglar by prying open a cannister of homemade German Christmas cookies I had spent hours making. The time I startled my dad so badly that he heaved himself and an iron skillet nearly through our wall, leaving a cartoonish fracture. (I think that one was the boys' favorite.)

"And that's what's so great about wallpaper, because you can just cover up funny cracks like that," I concluded. All at once I found Chandler's arms around my neck in an I-don't-want-to-ever-let-go hug.

"Thank you, Mommy, for all, every bits of those stories," he said. He gazed at me with a look of unqualified admiration, a look I last saw when I demonstrated that I really can touch the tip of my nose with my tongue. I could see that I had attained a new status in his eyes: I had once been five, too. Once upon a time I was a real little girl. For just a few moments he had slipped through a secret gate and stood alongside me as my playmate — known me as I was then. I held him close and understood better what Dr. James Dobson meant when he said:

We must tell them (our families) where we've been and how we got to this moment. Sharing about our faith, about our early family experiences, about the obstacles we overcame or the failures we suffered can bring a family together and give it a sense of identity. The stories of your past, of your child-hood, of the courtship with your spouse, etc. can be treasures to your children.[6]

◦◌◦ ◦◌◦ ◦◌◦

So where have I been and how did I get to this moment? How did you? Where to begin? Who has time to tell sto-ries, especially when life can get so crazy, barreling by like an express train? Sometimes I can drag my foot and slow the train, and sometimes it seems like I can't. But either way, I can at least look for some windows. Windows of opportunity.

Most days I don't have a serene 15 minutes at the dinner table to tell a leisurely story. Chances are, Ethan is making his jelly-laden bread crusts dance off the edge of his tray onto the carpet, the phone is shrilling and Chandy is abruptly hearing and heeding nature's call. Okay. So where is the window?

I'm learning that it's usually small—a skylight, not a picture window. Five minutes, not 15. And sometimes— no, most of the time—the window is a moving target. For example, when my husband sees me poring over my recipe box, I can take that moment to rave about the spiced peach jello or molasses crinkle cookies my mom used to stir up in our cheerful, blue-cabineted kitchen. When Chandler proudly scales the cherry tree, that might be just the moment to mention how his papa used to flee high into the refuge of tall firs every Saturday while his mom cleaned house and rattled the windows, playing her favorite opera music.

When a despondent friend sighs out the words, "Sometimes I wonder if I'll ever have a family...," maybe I can offer my memory of that steel-gray day when Alex and I said good-bye to our unborn baby and hello to a luminous rainbow arching right over our house. It seemed as if God was whispering to us, *Try again. I'm with you.* Then I can talk about how *Try again* became Ethan, our absolute joy of a boy.

I hope I always remember the window of opportunity that unexpectedly opened one afternoon at a bus stop on a rainy day. He looked young, too young to be shipping out the next day on a destroyer bound for the Persian Gulf. His story: His name was Jamal; he had just been trained in how to suit up for chemical warfare; he was scared. Our story: We understood being scared; we loved the Lord; we would pray for him and ask God to be with him.

Jamal's urgent eyes followed us as we left the bus; our prayers followed him into the war. We probably had less than five minutes with him. We don't know the rest of his story. But we know this: Little windows can let in a lot of light.

≈ ≈ ≈

Maybe you feel like you've never done much to talk about. You've never lived Hollywood high drama, the kind of scripted epic that has few real-life parallels. Good. That makes me feel better, because I haven't either.

No, I take that back. There was that morning when Ethan ran around with the bread hook from the mixer up his sleeve, looking very much like the infamous Captain Hook. That was pretty dramatic.

There was the time an ocean wave on a Maui beach swept me up in its frothy curl, tumbled me head over heels like a towel in a dryer and rudely spit me out on my chin onto sand. That was pretty suspenseful.

And there was that afternoon I dragged myself wearily home from work only to discover a perfect little basket of ivy and violets on my doorstep from a man I didn't even know cared for me. That was pretty touching... and suspenseful...and dramatic. Wasn't it? I mean, in a real-life kind of way.

Sometimes it is the smallest events, the simplest retellings, that touch and change lives. A story that may seem as common as the kitchen sink to me may be the very one that someone else never forgets.

Sometimes it's the smallest events, the simplest retellings, that touch and change lives.

Since we've mentioned kitchen sinks, let me suggest, for what it's worth, that there's a lot to be said for some of them. I read recently about an industrious homeowner who decided to renovate his 1927 bungalow. In the process, he pulled out the original cast-iron sink. As he tipped a leg to cart it out, he was startled by a sudden shower of silver dollars and half dollars. Long ago, an unknown someone had patiently stockpiled those coins in the leg, maybe for years. It occurs to me that it's possible for us to do something like that, too.

We can squirrel away our stories all our lives, for so many reasons. Maybe we're not sure we have anything important to say. Or we doubt if anybody's listening. Our stories may be stacked to the top of our hearts, and we just don't know what a treasure we have in there.

We would be as surprised as anyone else to find a cascade of silver memories showering out.

We might be amazed at what our memories could be worth to someone else. The way the honeysuckle vines around grandma's porch smelled. The loyal, floppy-eared dog with his fur nearly loved off. Our childhood hiding place. That trip of a lifetime. The first day as a new schoolteacher. The last day, surrounded by moving boxes, in the old house. And all the funny and sad, big and small experiences that say to us again and again that God has kept His promise to love us. Oh, what a treasure cache we have inside!

I've heard an old African proverb that says when an old person dies it's as if a library has burned down. That's the catch. What isn't passed to others doesn't last. The rich deposit of God in my life—my unique place in the cosmos, the laughter and hard-won lessons, my distinctive discoveries and triumphs, human and hopeful experiences—can vanish into a puff of smoke, a pile of ashes. I can live this life with too much unsaid; I can leave the same way, with the drawstring of my story bag pulled tight and secured with a knot. Or I can live with the drawstring looped in a bow, inviting others to read the pages of my life.

I can share my stories especially with those who live in my house, share my name and leave their sticky fingerprints all over my windows, walls, and heart. I can tell them the good things God has done for me. I must remember that the ones I love the most are the ones who most need to hear my stories. Not 5 or 10 or 20 years from now. They need to hear them now.

So I will tell Chandler and Ethan the stories of Jesus, those timeless truths that hold my soul steady. And I will tell them, too, God's loving story in me, this ordinary person who colors her hair, laughs over the Sunday comics, gets sad at the six o'clock news, ferries an eager boy back and forth to preschool, yearns to redo the bedroom and wonders about refinancing the house.

☙ ☙ ☙

This summer we passed a dubious household milestone: We had to have our septic tank opened up and pumped. Ethan, keenly interested, watched the aromatic proceedings from a safe distance. Then, because he was completely fascinated with holes in general, I held him as he peeked into that big dark underground tank. When he pointed and squealed with sudden recognition, saying, "That's the lions' den from Daniel!" I knew some of our stories were starting to stick.

With just two birthdays under his belt, he is already beginning to tell stories of his own. "I saw a toobertoothed tiger on the computer!" "'Member when Chandy fell into the cactus?" "'Member when the sweeper made the tablecloth on fire?" (a truly historic event that had happened the day before).

I do remember, especially the smoldering tablecloth. But even more important, Ethan remembers. Someday all those recountings and rememberings will hold him and Chandler close; those stories will be there for them when my arms no longer can be. Some of the stories will anchor them, some will give them wings. And at their very finest it is the stories, large and small, that will help lead them home to love. What a gift. What a wonder. And to think it's all in the bag.

Because I Love a Good Story...

My car clock glowed 2:00 A.M. as I drove down streets I still couldn't name. At least I wasn't lost again. I just didn't know where I was going. Not tonight. Not tomorrow. And that was the whole problem. When I had moved to the Pacific Northwest a year before, I felt God was launching me on a great adventure, a fresh start. There was so much to love about my new life—the daily exhilaration of new places and faces and opportunities, the natural beauty of the mountains and water, the incredibly early arrival of spring. But now the novelty of all the newness was beginning to wear thin.

I had done my best to appreciate seafood, to not get seasick on boats, to not get homesick at every turn. But how I longed for my doorbell or phone to ring. I was so tired of a table for one, a life for one. I didn't feel much like the conqueror of a brave new world anymore. I felt more like a lost and lonely pioneer trying to shield the embers of my campfire from being extinguished by the wind. I was so achingly far away from the hugs and laughter, the sturdy white farmhouses and cornfields of my Midwest home.

I was still trying to make sense of it all as I parked under a streetlight, switched off the engine and sat peering out at the deserted street and dark houses. I took a deep breath and faced the awful question again: *Lord, did I make the biggest mistake of my life in moving here, 3,000 miles away from everything and everyone I know and love?* I wasn't at all sure. But I was painfully sure of something else: There was no one in the whole world who knew where I was tonight, sitting alone in the dark, struggling to piece together my faith and my future. It was an overwhelming and terrifying thought, and I just put my head down on the steering wheel and let the tears come.

They were still coming when—bam! The impact bounced my car. I jerked bolt upright, my face wet with tears, my heart hammering in my throat. Staring through the windshield at me was a pair of enormous yellow eyes. They belonged to a huge, electrified cat—at least he looked electrified, with every bit of his long fur standing on end. He crouched frozen on my hood, looking for all the world like he'd just been aerial-dropped out of nowhere. He stared at me; I stared at him. I don't know which of us was more shocked.

It was comical, our eyeball-locked paralysis. I don't know what he thought of me, but I thought he looked like a weird combination of ultimate static and a bad-hair day. I had to laugh. Where in heaven's name had he come from?

"Hi there, kitty." I snuffled and loudly blew my nose. Cats. The apartment lease I had signed read "No pets allowed."

During my growing-up years there had always been at least one cat to make our house a home. A family needs a cat to drape a plumed tail in front of the TV screen when your favorite program is on, to claim the softest chair, pounce unexpectedly on toes coming around corners, or sun in a window and observe the world, pretending to be "queen" of the house.

In our house a cat participated in every season—eating the green plastic grass out of our Easter baskets; laying a tributary offering of one very dead bird on the sunny porch; diving into a just-raked pile of leaves; indignantly shaking a dusting of snow off chilly paws and heading for the warm register. Paw prints punctuated our family history.

I eased open the car door and slowly extended my hand. "Now, what are you doing here?" I asked. He could well have asked me the same question, but instead he stood up slowly and leaned tentatively into my hand. He didn't know a thing about me, young woman of the swollen eyes and red nose, but "cat lover" was the introduction he seemed to need. I petted him for a few minutes, then carefully picked him up and cuddled him a little. He wasn't a soft delicate fluffball; he was an unwieldy armful of rough softness. A tomcat was my unlikely companion in the night. I wondered if he knew where he had come from and where he was going. He did seem to know that he liked to have his ears scratched—just a little to the left, please.

I leaned up against the car, and for the next ten minutes or so, I just lost myself in scratching his ears, mummering silly things, holding him as tightly as he would allow. If he had somewhere to be or if this encounter seemed unusual to Mr. Cat at all, he kept it to himself and just lifted his nose and allowed his throat to be rubbed.

And that's all it was, just me petting a cat in the middle of a night that somehow didn't seem quite so dark anymore. And yet, that's not all it was, because some kind of a quiet miracle happened that night between me, God and this cat. You see, when I closed my eyes and hugged his warm solidness against me, something inside me stopped shaking. Something reached out across 3,000 miles and touched home. Something within me dropped anchor in dear, familiar ground and the anchor held.

Sometimes heaven doesn't open, and answers don't come in quite the way we expect. Sometimes comfort is better than an answer. It's been said that a bird sings not because it has answers but because it has a song. As I stood under that streetlight, hugging a cat, my homesickness was not permanently banished nor did I sprout instant Northwest roots. But I did feel that I was seen and embraced by a God who knows everything about me, right down to my love for cats. And that night I found my song again, a song of courage to go on.

My baby boy has his first tooth
and in most circles, that's not news.
News is that some stock is falling,
Or that a head of state is calling.
War and politics and drought—
now these are things to talk about.
So why do all those matters dim
with just one look at sweet, round him?
His little mouth, so often kissed . . .
that tiny bud of white we missed.
Stop all the presses!
This is news!
My baby boy has his first tooth!

DEENA LEE WILSON

✿

Earth's crammed with heaven
And every common bush afire with God.¹

ELIZABETH BARRETT BROWNING

Chapter Three

Treasure the Firefly
Moments

T'S A LITTLE THING, BUT A DELIGHT I REMEMBER WELL FROM CHILDHOOD. YOU NEED A BACKYARD AT SUMMERTIME DUSK, right at the cooling hour when stillness begins to descend and the muffled barks of dogs echo just a little. It helps if you can smell the last smoky embers in the barbecue grill or hear a revolving sprinkler's whispering hiss or the low hum of voices on a neighboring porch. You stand on one foot, then the other. Watching. Waiting.

Blink. You spy one tiny, teasing blink of lime-yellow light. On-off. Just that quick. Keep watching. There's another! On-off. A pinpoint flash, out by the peach tree. Then an answering blink from the corner of the shed...then by the clematis trellis...the fence...the garden...and right in front of your nose! *Blink-blink-blink-blink.*

In two minutes or less, as if on cue, the whole yard comes alive in a flashing network of lights. Those tiny winged creatures, each no bigger than a fat pencil lead, can set the night on fire. The dance of the fireflies has begun.

Fireflies. First tries. Little people a few feet high.

I sing the praises of things small. I can't help but notice that in our larger-than-life world, little things get overlooked and crowded out. In fact, it's easy to forget they have any value at all. Somehow, bigger always seems better. Mega-sizing reigns.

You know what I'd love to do sometime? Pull through a fast-food drive-through, and when that fuzzy voice (it's the same voice no matter where I go) blurts back to me, "Mummpghjgh?" which I intuitively know means "May I super-duper-size your order?" I'd like to say, "No, thanks. I'd like the tiniest bag of fries you have. Small is good." I can see that intercom falling off its post in a smoking heap.

Small is good. Very good. In fact I'm beginning to suspect that almost everything worth having starts small. I'm not sure why it comforts me so much to think that everything God does has a starting place, usually a humble one. One seed. One question. One choice. One prayer. One step.

I like the story Leonard Ravenhill tells of a group of tourists visiting a picturesque village. As they strolled along, they came upon an old man sitting on a fence. In a rather patronizing tone, one tourist asked, "Were any great men born in this village?" The old man contemplated for a moment and then said, "Nope. Only babies." Small seems a wonderful way to start not only people but just about anything.

These early years with our boys are full of little things and baby steps. Easily missed, luminous moments that flicker like fireflies. *Blink. Blink.* Like the day Chandler, flushed with excitement, announced, "I know how to do it, Mom!" He planted himself in front of me. "I can spell TV!" He was as proud as if he had just flown a strategic mission to the moon.

As we high-fived and I gave him a victory squeeze, I knew it wouldn't be any time at all until he would crack the secret code of the alphabet. Sooner or later (and probably sooner) all those funny symbols on street signs and billboards would begin to really mean something. Soon Alex and I would no longer be able to lapse into that mysterious dialect of the ancients (S-P-E-L-L-I-N-G). Soon our boy would be reading under his sheets to the glow of a flashlight after lights out. No matter that right now he still didn't quite know *k* from *q*.

On this day he had one little word. "Tomorrow" he would unlock an endless world of imagination and books. Such big doors can swing open on such little hinges. Even the doors of faith.

✿ ✿ ✿

When Chandler turned five, I began to wonder how I could introduce him to the practice of spending some personal time with God every day. Although our family talked about God in a natural way, all through our daily routine, didn't being five years old call for something more?

When he stumbled into our bedroom each morning— tousle-haired and sleepy-eyed—for his wake-up snuggle, it was a familiar sight for him to see me propped up in bed with my Bible on my knees, my big pink glasses on my nose, and my notecards, pen and highlighter strewn about. (Except on mornings that came too soon, when he observed me stretched prone, face-down, gasping, "Was that supposed to be a night?")

Beyond my fairly consistent example of a devotional life, I pondered what else I could do. Maybe read a short Bible story with him each morning? Memorize a new scripture each week? Have a short prayer together? Reality crystallized my noblest plans down to this: We snuggle. Chandler wiggles, giggles and chatters beside me on the mountain of pillows, and sometime during this wiggling-giggling-chattering process, I say (or shout), "God, the day is new and we love You!"

Sometimes this proclamation is made more difficult by the fact that Chandler is sitting on my stomach, but on the best days we even manage to say it in unison. Okay, so it isn't the Moody Bible Hour, but it is a sweet start to the day. It isn't hushed, but it is holy. I'll not only take it, I'll treasure it.

It seems to me that real life is so often lived in the minor key of little things and small starts like this. I have yet to understand how God takes everyday details and time and polishes them up into warm memories, but somehow He does.

☪ ☪ ☪

As someone once said, isn't it a wonder that when we look back on our lives, some of the things that matter the most seem almost too small to talk about? Oh, yes. Things like the smile lines around the corners of my husband's incredibly blue eyes. Or the way a new book feels in my hands when I press it open for the first time. Or the sound of my sister laughing over the phone about some silly thing I said. Or the heady, exotic scent of the lily blooming outside my kitchen window. Or the delightful discovery I made as a new mom that there's a spot right under the curve of my jaw just made for nestling a baby's downy head.

Granted, these may not seem like things to write home about. But they are things that write "home" on my heart. "The soap in the bathroom, the flowers in the garden, the book on the bedside table are all strong symbols of a life in progress," observes writer Charlotte Moss. "You look at these details and a world unfolds."[2] Well, I'm often too busy folding a mountain of laundry to think about worlds unfolding. But my heart understands just what she means.

It is the "trivialities" that are my daily emotional touchstones. The milestones—Ethan's second birthday, our ninth anniversary, the family vacation to Phoenix— may fill my photo albums. But it is really the touchstones, the little things, that nourish my soul. Maybe Fanny Fern said it best: "There are no little things. Little things, so called, are the hinges of the universe."[3] They certainly seem to be the hinges of my universe.

I hope my sons will grow up talking about hinges. I hope they never feel that the little things that have mattered most to them may be too small to talk about. It's a perplexing reality, I've heard other parents say, but some of the things that make up your child's unforgettable memories may be things they somehow never even think to tell you.

I know some of the scenes I will revisit years from now, the everyday moments that will always say to me with tenderness, "Yes, that's how life was then. That's how we were then."

Chandler loudly singing, "I Just Can't Wait to Be King!" and meaning it.

Ethan, stationed behind a huge, empty ice cream glass, his smeared face a testimony to ecstasy and supreme accomplishment.

Sesame Street. Our street. Ethan's feet...as sturdy and square as shoe boxes.

Chandler, hanging a dozen Christmas tree ornaments on one groaning branch.

Us pulling the van over (again) to show Ethan all the "big diggers" at construction sites.

Me, trying to fix dinner on the same counter where a dad and two boys are eagerly offering a Venus flytrap its first feast—one very dead fly.

Peanut butter (lots of it).

Sleep (never enough of it). Uninterrupted conversation (What is it?).

Papa's good pancakes. Birthday cakes. The marathon stamina parenting takes.

"I had it first!" "Wait for me!" "Mommmmmy! I'm talking to you...."

Ethan, his dark little head bent intently over a book bigger than he is.

Chandler with his big Fisher-Price castle permanently attached to one foot (don't even ask).

Owies. Things that go bump in the night. Hellos and good-byes.

Summer haircuts. Bug jars. Sprinklers.

Chandler checking daily to see what color socks to wear to match Papa's socks. (Me, wiping away a happy-sad tear. He won't grow up to be like me.)

Both boys bursting in with weird "knock-em-dead" breath from grazing on the chives and mint in the backyard.

McDonalds together. The zoo together. The library together. Life together.

It seems that no matter how grown-up I become, small things still matter. Thirty years later I still know just how to insert my key and lift and jiggle the temperamental front doorknob of my childhood home where my parents still live. I must have done it a million times growing up.

❧ ❧ ❧

"We're replacing our siding, you know." My mom's voice came across the phone line as she gave me a long-distance update on their latest remodeling projects. "The front entrance, screen door, everything's going to be new." She sounded new and bright, anticipating this long-awaited facelift for the home in which she and Dad had raised the five of us.

"The front door is going too, then?" I asked, hearing the forced nonchalance in my voice. "The—uh—doorknob? Everything?" I blinked back sudden, unexpected tears. I was glad she couldn't see me.

Long story short, we ended up talking about the old front door key I've carried on my key chain almost all my life, even since moving cross-country 15 years ago.

About a week after our conversation, a small beige envelope arrived in the mail. Across the front was a note in my mom's dear, familiar handwriting. "You've always had the key to our hearts," it read. "Now here is the key to our house." Out fell a new shiny gold key. She's a mom. She understands.

❧ ❧ ❧

And then there are the baby steps. I can't help but notice that I never seem to move too far away from them. Somewhere inside each of us I think we must instinctively know that real life is rarely lived in giant strides or grand opportunities. Most of us don't really believe that we're going to be an overnight success at something or that we'll lose 10 pounds by tomorrow or buy the house of our dreams next week or that we'll bond with our children in one weekly session of quality time. "Real life," observed Leo Tolstoy, "is lived when small changes occur."[4] Those firefly moments. So easily missed. *Blink. Blink.*

"Mommy...Mommy, watch me!"

"Can we read that again?"

"I did it!"

"Let me see. Let me try. Let me help."

"Can you show me how?"

And even in love (or maybe, especially in love!), small things are the rudders that turn mighty ships. I was reminded of that again last week when a three-hooked clothes rack fell off the wall in the boys' bedroom. You just never appreciate something until it's gone. All at once I had this crumpled pile of orphan pajamas, T-shirts and jeans with no place to live.

"Can we just put this thing somewhere until I can fix it?" Alex said as he held up the rack with the two lonely-looking screws still dangling from the back.

I sighed with exasperation. "Could we just stick

it back in the wall for now? It's wobbly, but it works."

"Let me fix it right away," Alex replied. He disappeared into the garage, whistling cheerfully.

I basked for a moment in the warmth of those wonderful words. I was incredulous. He had said, "Let me fix it right away." So why did I hear, "I love you"? What subtle shifts and changes in our nine-year marriage had metamorphosed me into a woman who heard love's voice in a completed task, not just in a sweet note on my windshield or a rose on my nightstand? (I still like those things too, by the way.) When did it happen? It wasn't a single event with a beginning and end, like dinner or a breaking news story. Instead I think it happened progressively, as the ripples from Alex's small pebbles of everyday service — lugging trash, rinsing dishes, running the vacuum — have come lapping up on my shores.

Ten years ago it would have seemed very unromantic to me, but now I think Erma Bombeck knew her stuff when she wrote, "Love is a lot of little things that add up to caring. It doesn't always add up to three little words. Sometimes it adds up to six: I got your tank filled today."[5]

Yes, love is a lot of little things. Layers of living. Oft-repeated acts. Fragments, moments, choices that somehow compound into a cohesive whole as solid as a rock.

Love is being faithful to pray for five available minutes, believing that God hears me and will work wonders even when that guilty voice in my head shrieks that I should give up if I can't pray for at least a half hour.

Love is going out in the yard and being the chief bubble-blower when I'm longing to just lounge and read about spring wreaths in my new magazine.

Love is sometimes not being the chief bubble-blower, so that I can read my magazine instead and show my boys that mommies need down time, too.

Love is taking one full minute to kneel down and give my son a prolonged adoring gaze.

Love is doing my best to listen when the questions are something like, "What if my whole body was just eyeballs?" "If a volcano blew up in our bathroom sink, would it make new land?" "Is coleslaw an animal?"

Love is remembering that in the middle of nose wiping, tear drying, shoe tying, and diaper buying, there is a God bending close to see each humble offering.

Love is taking a second to cut a smiley face into the bologna slices for lunch, not because it will rock the world but because it will make two little boys giggle, and laughter lingers.

Love is remembering that in the middle of nose wiping,

tear drying, shoe tying, and diaper buying, there is a God bending close to see each humble offering.

☖ ☖ ☖

On weary days when it seems there is more whining than wonder, more negotiating than nurturing, it's good to remember the widow woman from Jesus' day. Do you know who I mean? The one whose two foolish pennies barely made a clink as she dropped them into the temple offering box...the one who turned Jesus' head as He said to His disciples something like this, "Do you see that woman? The sound of her two pennies in the box is ringing all the bells and whistles of heaven."

When I think of her, I think of the words of Mother Teresa of Calcutta, "We can do no great things, only small things with great love."[6] There you go. Little things with largeness of heart. That's what I want to do.

Heaven knows I've never cradled the destitute and dying of India in my arms as Mother Teresa did. But I have knelt down in the grass with my son, beside a very still sparrow, and looked into a little face shadowed by the first questions about death. I've never washed out my dress in a metal bucket at night like Mother Teresa did, but I've scrubbed up substances that would make some grown men buckle at the knees. I may never win an award for peace, but I will do my best to teach two brothers the beauty of respect and caring, starting with today's little lesson: sharing the cheese crackers. I don't know that I'll ever change the world for thousands. But I will change the world for two little boys who call me Mommy, who will shoot like living arrows for the Lord into a time I will never see.

And they are why I'm learning to cherish the small yet significant lasting things—for them. But most of all for Him—for Jesus—who drew a probably sweaty little child with dirty fingernails close to Him and said, "Look. Here is what it's like to be the greatest in the kingdom of heaven."[7]

I am standing in the crowd that day and I can almost hear Him saying to me, "Remember what counts. Little things and little people weigh heavy in the scales of heaven. Remember what it was like to be this size when wonder came so easily. Remember how it felt to always be looking up."

How we need to keep looking up to Jesus, especially all of us who are up to our eyeballs in little things, day after day, sometimes wondering with a sigh if such trivial stuff can possibly matter. How we need to keep encouraging each other to do the small things with great love. To push the playground swing a little longer. To take a deep breath and answer yet another "Why, Mommy?" To tickle and be silly. To give time for just one more roll down the hill. To fly the kite until the string breaks.

Deep inside we know the truth: The lights of love and relationship don't snap on like a floodlight at the flip of a magic switch. They twinkle on—one at a time—like stars, like the fireflies glowing from the unexpected corners of a still summer night. So we go on giving in a thousand little ways each day. And then we get to watch and wait. And we'll see it there in the hearts of those we love. *Blink. Blink. Blink.* The lights of a lifetime are twinkling on.

🐝 🐝 🐝

As I drove home from a round of errands in the van one day, Chandler suddenly pointed out the side window and exclaimed, "Mommy! Look!" Hopping in the dusty berm was a fat robin with a crimson breast and a beak full of straw. For a second there was something about the afternoon light—a radiance that made that little bird look magnified, lit from inside, its beak stuffed with spun gold. I was sure the robin had pecked a hole and escaped from the pages of a beautiful children's storybook. For Chandy and I, it was an instant of shared wonder. Then the traffic light changed and we drove on.

It hardly seems possible to me now, but I know the time we spend as a family under one roof will be fleeting. Before we know it, the light will change, and everything

and everyone will move. But for now, if we have the eyes
to see them, there are simple moments together for giving, for applauding little victories, for sharing our baby
steps toward greater things, for discovering that in the
end it is the small things that are the great things after all.
As we treasure these moments, we will be lit from inside
by a light that lasts and a love that stays—the love of our
God, who cherishes all things, great and small.

Because I Love a Good Story…

Dear Ethan,

I wanted to tell you, little son, about your first prayer
so that you will always know.

I am a writer, just like every other mom or dad
(though most of us don't think of ourselves that way).
I'm not writing a short story or even a novelette. The
story I give myself to every day is a novel, joyfully long
in the telling. I think it will take a lifetime, at least.

I am not writing it the way you watch me write each
morning, squinting at my computer screen, tapping per-
sistently at the keyboard, or maybe scratching my head
with a pencil and staring into space. And I'm not even
writing most of this story on paper, the kind you so enjoy
scribbling circles on or using for cutting practice. This

story is being written in you, Ethan—a day, a chapter, a shared experience at a time. Each time I say "Oh, I remember when…" and go on to tell you a story—about that wonderful day you were born, or why we chose your name, or how you uniquely grew or why you are an irreplaceable part of all that makes us a family—I add to the unfolding story in you.

I'll let you in on a secret, son. Someday the little stories I tell you about yourself may quietly do big things. They may help you discover who you are, where you have come from, where you belong. For now your papa and I are the keepers and tellers of your stories, especially in these early years. But someday you will own your stories. They will be as much a part of you as your bones, shaken down to your toes, imprinted in every part of you. I hope they become a treasure you never leave home without. As unique as your fingerprint, your "Story of Me" will be yours to tell, yours to love and yours to continue. So let me say "I remember when…" and tell you this story about your first prayer.

You had said "Yes" in a breathy voice just above a whisper. You pushed the still-new word out carefully, like blowing a fragile bubble that might pop in your face. I asked you the question while on my knees beside you as you sat in your high chair, swallowed by an oversized bib. I wasn't on my knees because it felt like a holy moment. I was there because your peanut butter sandwich for lunch was ready and because it was time to pray as we did every mealtime. Kneeling down on your eye-level was easier on my overworked back than bending down so far to grasp your little hand.

Usually we were a circle of three—you, your brother Chandler and I. But today Chandler was enjoying playing like a big boy at a friend's house while I took you to the pediatrician for your 18-month-old checkup. This was my chance to look at embraceable you undistracted: your companionable round face, your ready, welcoming smile, your "power build"—sturdy arms and legs on a square trunk—so much like your Grandpa Duncan. Dr. O'Grady peeked and peered at you, squeezed and gently thumped you like a melon and proclaimed you healthy. In my heart, for the millionth time, I proclaimed you a wonder and a joy.

So now we were back home for lunch, me feeling buoyant and you, no doubt, feeling hungry. Usually you and Chandler and I joined hands and Chandler prayed, but since Chandler was gone, I half teasingly turned to you and asked, "Do you want to say the blessing, baby?" That was when you made me do a double take by whispering "Yes." Yes, you would say the blessing (whatever that was).

Maybe in those pre-two-year-old days, saying yes just came more easily to you than saying no. But there you sat, ready and available, your plump little legs crossed at the ankles. It was as if both your peanut butter sandwich and your "Yes" were now sitting right on the high chair tray in front of you, and you were equally pleased with both. I had the feeling that you were now expecting to watch this thing called The Blessing happen to you. Having been invited, now it was going to come toward you or upon you the way Mommy's kisses or the big warm washcloth or the soft breeze from the kitchen window did.

Although you had heard a lot of prayers in your year and a half in our family, I had never heard you say a prayer. As I remember, your vocabulary at this point would have made one very thin dictionary; it was pretty well exhausted by "yes," "no," "Mama" and "Papa." We were still anticipating what your voice was really going to sound like once we could hear more of it at one time.

On any other day, I might have heard your "Yes," smiled, ruffled your hair and then gone ahead and said the blessing myself. But today seemed like a day for lingering a little. I just wanted to wander down this unexpected pathway with you and see where it might lead us. So I bowed my head as if you said the blessing every day of the week and knew just what to do. And I waited.

Silence. For about 10 seconds. I cracked open one eye and you were watching me. You sat still as a mouse, your brown eyes big with uncertainty and expectation, your lips parted slightly. *Is it coming?* your expression seemed to say. *Is The Blessing almost here?*

"Baby, do you have any words to say to God?"

"No." You were matter-of-fact, unapologetic.

Well, I was just checking. I don't know what I expected you to say. "Yes, mother. I have been wanting to fully speak my mind for some time, but I just didn't know where to begin."

No, of course not. It's just that babies change almost as quickly as their diapers do and they're always catching their moms by surprise. I wanted to make sure that you hadn't been teasing me, hiding a complete vocabulary somewhere in your back pocket.

I hesitated. Why did it seem as though I was feeling my way by braille, question by question, along a wall toward an open, sunlit doorway of possibility?

"Umm, could you sing to God, then, Ethan? Like this?" I sounded a note.

"Yes." You didn't move a muscle. Maybe you didn't even blink.

"Okay then. Good." I closed my eyes, bowed my head again and felt the small weight of your hand in mine, soft and warm and trusting. The clock in the living room ticked softly. There was a silence so expectant it seemed somehow full—round with promise. And then I heard you, Ethan.

You sang a note.

One high, sweet, perfect note.

Heaven opened and The Blessing came.

I wonder if the angels elbowed and shushed each other and stilled their music.

I wonder if your Grandma Wilson in heaven brushed away a tear. (I know I did.) I wonder if Jesus turned and said, "Ah, there's my Ethan. Yes, that's my boy's voice...."

You didn't have a lot to give God that day, Ethan, but you gave Him what you had. As you grow, remember that how much you have to give isn't important. Just give God whatever you can out of whatever you have; that is what delights Him most.

Do you know that God is always at work in His world for good? Jesus said, "My Father is always doing good, and I am following His example." This means that all around you there will always be those who are stepping toward God, searching to find a piece of Him, a place in Him, for the very first time. Inside you, too, God will always be starting some fresh, marvelous work.

God's sweet breeze will be moving through all your life's turns and changes. "The wind blows where it will," the Bible says, "and no one knows on whom God will next bestow this wonderful life from heaven." Listen for God's wind, Ethan. Let it blow on you. Go where it goes, son.

When you feel afraid or alone or discouraged, remember God. Remember His goodness. Be patient and gentle with people. Help them find their place and their voice in God. Be a safe harbor where they can find the courage to trust and try. And be very glad with them in their small beginnings, as I was with you that day.

So much has changed since the day of your first prayer. Now you are almost three and you have a river of words. We no longer wonder what your voice will sound like. You speak well enough to ask politely for more "cannonballs" (my meatballs) and to excitedly inform the world that "a crocodile bit my foot!" When you can be persuaded to sit still for a moment, you pray for everything from Grandma to the water sprinkler to hot dogs to dinosaurs.

There will never be another time quite like the time when you made your first innocent reach toward God. But there will be time and time and time again to discover Him all your life long. Always give God your beautiful first note, Ethan. And just as I did that day, your mom will hear a symphony.

I love you, my little son.

Mom

We have only this moment,
sparkling like a star in our hand...
and melting like a snowflake.[1]

MARIE BENYON RAY

Each day opens and closes like a flower.[2]

JOHN MUIR

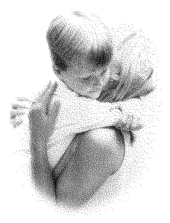

Chapter Four

Find the Tenth Step

I WONDER IF YOU'VE EVER MET OWL, CREATED BY CHILDREN'S BOOK AUTHOR ARNOLD LOBEL. OWL HAS AN UPSTAIRS and downstairs in his house with 20 steps on the stairway. When Owl is downstairs, he wonders how his upstairs is. When he is upstairs, he wonders how his downstairs is getting along. Finally he decides that if he runs very fast he can be both places at the same time.

He gets his feathers in a flurry as he runs and runs and runs. "Faster! Faster! Faster!" he cries to himself as he sprints up and down the staircase. Finally he runs right into his defining moment: the realization that he can never run fast enough.

"When I am up, I am not down. When I am down, I am not up. All I am is very tired!" And with that, he plops himself down on the tenth step, because it is the step right in the middle.

I searched half my life for that tenth step, the place where I could finally stop running and sit down squarely in the moment.

I think I have quite a bit in common with Owl. Maybe you do, too. It is an effort for me to sit down and remember that the tenth step—the here and now—is both a gift and a destination. Life is always happening today. Yet sometimes I miss out on the newness of life because I don't stay in the nowness of life.

So often, rather than being present, I am in pursuit—up and down life's staircase. (Or, as it sometimes seems, up the down staircase!) I'm worried about tomorrow's doctor appointment or yesterday's grocery bill. I wonder when and how we will find a bigger house. I overload just thinking about how I'll ever dig out from under the never-ending list of things to be done. I lament the sad reality that once I do get something done, it so quickly undoes itself.

"Nobody steps on this clean floor!" I simultaneously plead and command as my sons burst through the door, bringing half the soil in the yard with them on their jeans. (I may or may not notice the bedraggled dandelion bouquets both boys have in their fists.) Up the steps, down the steps I go. It is so easy for me to mistake all that motion for progress. At night I fall into bed like a stone. Like Owl, I end up bone tired.

"Tomorrow," penned poet Pearl Phillips, "is never promised earthly man, nor does it often fit a plan. Today...is gold that covers hills and dell, and rich are those who use it well."[3]

I think Jesus was a man who knew how to use each day well. He was so rich, though he grew up hammering his thumb in an "I think we just missed it" kind of town. Surely He had His own staircase that He could have run up and down, too. Maybe He could have spent His whole life longingly reflecting on how glorious it was to be shoulder-to-shoulder with His Father in heaven. Certainly He could have spent countless hours consumed by the brevity of the life He would enjoy and the dread of the future for which He was destined—the agony of the cross. But look at Jesus. Look at Him that starry Bethlehem night. When His little, red baby heels touched the hay, the creator of all eternity humbled Himself to a life that would unfold exactly as ours do, one day at a time. Maybe that was one of the greatest miracles of all.

And look at Him in His daily routine. Look at the sense of rest and rhythm that was the hallmark of both the mundane and the miraculous moments of His life.

Author Tim Hansel confesses:

I don't understand how the Master could take time to go alone into the desert to fast and pray when the whole world was starving and in chaos, when countless individuals needed Him.... I don't understand how He could say that sometimes it is better just to sit at His feet than to be up doing things for Him.... Or how He could ask us to be like little children when the world needs more firm leadership and harder workers. I don't understand how Jesus could play and celebrate and enjoy life when the world was in the condition it was in. I don't understand...but He did.[4]

I'm with Mr. Hansel. I don't understand either, but I want to. I want my life to be rich with meaning the way Jesus' life was. I want to live each today well. I want to remember that God, the great I Am, is with me every moment of every day. I want to believe that the gift of time He has given me each new day—24 hours, 1,440 minutes, 86,400 seconds—is just the time I need to achieve His loving purposes for my life.

Is it because I'm in my forties that I'm so aware of this? Is it because I see my choices in almost instant replay on the faces and in the actions and reactions of my two little sons? I'm not sure. But I wonder how it changes me when I begin to believe that there's something rich in every moment to be experienced. I wonder what happens inside me as I learn to live each day as if it were something irreplaceable, a fresh canvas every 24 hours.

Maybe one of the reasons Jesus lived life so well is because He understood right from the manger that the ordinary was one of God's favorite places to be.

ণ্ড ণ্ড ণ্ড

Have you discovered, as I have, that the gold of today comes cleverly concealed in the crumpled brown bag of everydayness? Come on now. Even for the most poetic of us, it takes a lot of imagination (or maybe inspiration) to see something holy in the humdrum of everyday routine — phone calls, vet visits, cold sores, laundry, grocery runs.

The future can be so alluringly dressed up and the past has strange ways of reinventing itself each time I visit. But the now? Now is reality's address, warts and all. *Now* the van needs fixing. Those post-baby pounds need to be shed. Now is the words, "Honey! The toilet paper is all gone!" Some days it's easy to want to fly away. Surely real life is happening beyond the next bend. Dale Turner writes:

> The real thing is always going on somewhere else. When you are young, you think it will come later. Later on, you think it was earlier. When you are here, you think it is there. When you get there, you find that life has doubled back and is quietly waiting here, here in the place you ran away from.[5]

I've done my share of running, haven't you? It's always something. When I was single, standing alone with my hands in my pockets as I watched a sunset big enough for two, the real thing was to be married. When I was married and the tears came because the babies didn't, the real thing was to have a child. When the long-awaited baby arrived and sleep departed, the real thing was to have just five minutes of free time to stand alone watching a sunset. And on and on. You can probably fill in the blanks with your own story, your personal pursuit of the real thing.

So where does that leave us? It leaves me ready to have the real thing now. It leaves me ready to begin living fully today. It makes me ready to believe that even when a season of life, a day or a moment isn't magical, it is still deeply meaningful simply because it is God's gift to me.

And speaking of gifts...a few Christmases ago my husband did a double take as he passed another car. The backseat of the other vehicle was piled high with brightly wrapped packages, but that's not what caught his eye. It was the woman at the wheel. She was systematically ripping open gifts as she drove, tossing them aside after a cursory glance and then grabbing for the next one. In a flurry of wrapping paper and ribbon and presents, she just kept rolling down the road. Heaven knows what she was doing. Had she just robbed a charity collection of toys for kids? Did she have a slew of relatives who gave her white elephant gifts? Was the little girl inside her acting on a long-suppressed urge to rip open all her presents before Christmas morning? I haven't a clue.

One thing I'm quite sure of. She couldn't possibly have been paying attention to where she was going or what she was doing. I can envision her standing before a judge, a scrap of Christmas wrap still caught in her hair. "No, sir. I honestly didn't see that light. Siren? I never heard it. Stop sign? Well, there was just no way I could stop."

The thought occurs to me that I don't want to be like her. I don't want to someday hear myself confessing, "First tooth? No, I honestly didn't see it. He was asking me questions? Gosh, I guess I missed them. She needed a friend? Well, there was just no way I could stop."

I want to stop. I want to see, really see. I want to listen and learn. I want to play and relax. I want to occupy my moments and cherish each today as if it will never be again. Because it never will be. I don't want to rip through moment after moment with those I love, always assuming that when I turn around, somewhere in the backseat there will always be more — more time someday when I'm not so preoccupied; more experiences; more opportunities. More gifts. More todays.

I want to respond to Paula D'Arcy's invitation, "Drink fully of life and people and places. This is your day. Life is the gift. And it is good."[6]

I want to say yes to life just as it is today.

◈ ◈ ◈

Just this year my mother told me a story about the twilight year of my grandma's life. She died when I was nine years old. A warm, compassionate woman despite the chronic pain of crippling arthritis, Bertha Gallatin mothered four daughters through the Depression years. At the close of her life she was bedridden by arthritis and by breast cancer that had eaten its way through her bones. Still she said yes to life.

Some days I feel like a very small boat on a very big sea of priorities, and it's a stretch just to make sure everyone is breathing and nobody is floating a slipper in the toilet.

She said it by being delighted over the upcoming arrival of my mom's fifth child, my youngest brother. Grandma thumbed through magazines, snipping out a picture of a round baby with dark hair. Surely, she told Mom with anticipation, this was what her new grandbaby would look like.

She said yes again by eagerly perusing the floor plans for her oldest daughter's new house. She didn't live to cuddle the new baby or to see the new house built. But she did leave a gift of herself—the affirmation that each day of life, even when mixed with pain and uncertainty, is still good. That even in the face of death, today and now is the only place to be fully alive. Her example testifies to me across the years, like a shining footprint of faith.

I need inspiration like that. There are so many days when I feel like a very small boat on a very big sea of priorities and demands. See each day as a gift? There have been days when it's a stretch just to make sure everyone is breathing and nobody is floating a slipper in the toilet.

My options about how the day unfolds can seem very limited. But I am beginning to clue in to something that is helping me to reclaim some time I was sure I didn't have. Like a million other multitasking moms, there are moments when I really do need to make a sandwich, give a hug, adjust my pantyhose and jot a phone number down all at the same time. But there are other times—probably lots of them—when I am being swept along by pure inertia. I'm in motion, so I remain in motion. As I become aware of this, I'm beginning to give myself the luxury of doing just one thing at a time when I can. This return to single-mindedness is like sinking down into the welcome shade of a personal oasis.

I'm also learning to think a radical thought as I face irritations, inconveniences, interruptions and unfinished tasks. Could they sometimes be heavenly summonses in disguise, invitations to relationship with God and His life, to things that are lasting? Could they be the unlikely *X* on the treasure map of life?

When it feels as though life and people are in my way

and I'm beginning to feel hostile, do I need to stop, look and listen? I'm finding that when I do, it is almost like I've built an altar and lit a welcoming candle in the middle of my everydayness. And sometimes it's as if God comes down all over again, right down into the "hay" of a common moment.

〜 〜 〜

The day Raggedy Andy was baptized, I was chopping and slicing at the kitchen counter while Chandler, four at the time, sat at the table absorbed in his book.

"Mommy," he said, "who is this?"

I glanced at the picture he held up. "That's John the Baptist."

"John the who?"

"The Baptist." There was the predictable pause, followed by the inevitable next question.

"What's Baptist?" His blue eyes were intent.

I hesitated. "Well, Baptist is a name that means he was a man who baptized." I would have done just fine if Chandler had let it go at that.

"What's baptize?"

I took a deep breath and gave it my best effort. "If you love Jesus, you need to be baptized. That means they put you under the water—"

As I remember, his alarmed expression told me he was

probably making some unpleasant connections: Baptism means being dunked and getting water up your nose.

I hurried to clarify. "You go under, but then you come up again."

He looked a little relieved but no less confused. I laid down the knife and tried again. "Being baptized is a way of showing that you've become a new person inside. So you go down in the water—" *No, no.* I could see I was losing him on this underwater thing.

Admittedly, it did sound pretty strange, like a mild form of torture. First the poor baptizee gets dunked, then he gets water shot up his nose, and to top it off he resurfaces with an identity crisis, as a "new person." *O—kay.*

I bought myself time by doing something like extra-vigorous chopping. Was it really so important to define baptism right now? How much could a preschooler understand anyway? This seemed like an excellent time for me to make a quick exit from the conversation. "Seemed" is the operative word. Short of someone showing up with the Jaws of Life to extract me, I knew I wouldn't get off so easily. But I was sorely tempted to just blurt out the grown-up definition—that baptism is an "outward sign of a inward change"—and leave it at that. Then I could stick my head in the refrigerator and begin rummaging busily.

You see, four years into motherhood, I was not naive enough to think that every moment had to be a teachable one. There were plenty of times when things were crazy and questions needed to be put on hold. But somehow this time was different. Notions of escape and feelings of inadequacy aside, I really wanted to be the one to help Chandler understand. But it would take some time. And I just didn't know how to do it.

That's when I noticed the Raggedy Andy doll. Raggedy had been tossed aside in play and had collapsed, exhausted but still smiling, in a colorful heap against our pine dish cupboard.

"Chandy, do you know where Ethan's Raggedy Andy is?"

He looked startled. "Uh-huh, but—"

"Would you just run and get it for me?"

Twin Raggedy Andys lived at our house, compliments of Aunt Bobbie. A handmade labor of love, one had arrived for each boy's first Christmas. The dolls were nearly identical, about 30 inches tall with blue pants, red plaid shirts and tangles of bright red yarn hair.

By the time Chandler returned, dragging Raggedy by one arm, I was a woman on a mission. Dolls in hand, we marched down the hallway and into our bathroom. Chandler's mouth made a little O of surprise as I stepped into the bathtub.

"Come on in," I invited, holding out my arms to him. "I'm going to show you what baptizing is. Let's pretend the tub is full of water."

If Chandler was thinking that maybe Mommy had been cooped up just a little too long, he never let on. Eyes bright with excitement, he scrambled into the tub.

He was watching like a hawk as I set my Raggedy on the edge of the tub and took his cloth hands in mine.

"Now Raggedy," I said, looking deep into the doll's unblinking eyes. "Do you love Jesus with all your heart?"

"Yes, I do," Raggedy said in a sincere, squeaky voice.

"And would you like to be baptized to show your love for Jesus?"

"Yes, I would!" Raggedy was a very enthusiastic new believer.

I led Raggedy to the center of the tub, putting one of my hands over his black embroidered nose and one behind his back for support.

"Raggedy," I proclaimed with great feeling, "I baptize you now in the name of the Father, the Son and the Holy Spirit—one God!" I dipped Raggedy backwards and the most surprising thing happened.

No bells chimed. No music played. No tidal wave of emotion or eerie sense of the supernatural swept over me. Raggedy simply went under. And the very real presence of the Lord simply came down. It felt as natural as another person stepping into the room. Jesus was suddenly close, suddenly with us as we stood there in that tub—a mom and her boy in the middle of a funny, impromptu object lesson with two mop-headed dolls.

It was as if He was whispering approvingly, "Yes. Oh, yes."

When I stood Raggedy back up on his feet, his arms shot high in the air. He was exuberant, full of the joy of the Lord. "Thank you, Jesus!" he squeaked.

Chandler pressed in eagerly, no longer content to be an observer. "Okay, let me do it. It's my turn now!"

He stepped forward; I stepped back. He positioned his Raggedy Andy on the edge of the tub, asked the questions as best he could remember them and tried to carefully repeat what I had done. As he dipped his doll back into the imaginary water, my mind shot ahead 10, 15, 20 years. All at once I didn't see a little boy with chubby hands and size four jeans dunking his doll in the tub. I saw the man he would someday be—a man walking with God, loving Him and knowing His ways. Because of thousands of common, easy-to-miss moments like this one. In my heart I whispered, *Thank You, Lord. I just don't think it gets any better than this.*

But maybe it does. Because what has been said is true: When I'm teaching my son, I'm also teaching my son's sons. That could be a whole lot of people to fit into our tub. But it's just the right number to fit into God's kingdom. I don't want to be too busy, too preoccupied, too tired to be available to God and to those I love. I know I won't do it all perfectly, but I want to be there to deposit in my little sons' hearts memories like this one, moments that the Holy Spirit will catch hold of to draw them Godward for the rest of their lives.

Yes, my life is full of complications and countless distractions. Yours may be, too. I have this funny feeling that our world may never return to simpler times. But maybe rather than longing for simpler times, we can simply look to Jesus to help us become people who understand what our time is for.

Maybe we can say with assurance, as the psalmist did, "My times are in your hands."[7] Perhaps we can say with our lives, as Jesus did, that the time we have is just the time we need to accomplish God's loving purposes for us.

Best of all, maybe we can choose to stop running up and down our staircases and sit down firmly on our "tenth step" to discover that the often ordinary here and now is the best place for us. It's the place of relationship, aliveness, availability. The place of divine possibilities. Then I think we will know a little something about being wise. Maybe even as wise as an owl.

Because I Love a Good Story...

I answered my doorbell one day and found myself face-to-face with a member of the UJP: the Unfinished Jobs Patrol. She was a commanding presence, with her very muscled arms, her very white teeth and her very clean fingernails. Her hair was twisted back in a knot so tight it matched the one in my stomach.

"Just spot-checking the neighborhood," she said crisply. Her eyes probed beyond my shoulder into the toy-littered entryway. "Made any progress on those baby books yet? Family photo album? Breakfast dishes? Bathroom floor?"

I took a small step backward, swallowing hard. "Well...I guess they're coming along," I stammered.

She sighed and shook her head. "Just as I thought. What has happened to you since you've become a mom? You used to be such a finisher. You used to dot every *i* and cross every *t*. Oh, the things you accomplished. What — ?"

"Mommmyyy!" Chandler wailed. He appeared at my elbow, a green plastic sand bucket on his head for protection. "Ethan is hitting...hard." He tugged on my sleeve. "Can we do that science thing again where juice eats the dirt off pennies?"

"Maybe later," I murmured.

My visitor reasserted her presence. "As I was saying, this is not a social call. There are some serious charges against you. Tampering."

"Tampering?" I was dumbfounded.

"I'm afraid so." She flipped open a little notebook. "Tampering with your to-do list. It appears that you have deliberately added silly items to your list, just so you can cross something off as done." She thrust her incriminating little notebook under my nose, jabbing at it with her pen. "Do you call these valid to-do entries? Get out of bed? Open your eyes? Begin to breathe?"

I felt weak. It was as if my whole previously organized life was passing before my eyes. Honestly, I had never intended to become a lady of perpetual nonclosure. Somehow it had just happened, one little unreturned phone call, one dirty diaper, one new baby at a time.

"You have become shameless," she snapped. "So desperate to accomplish some small thing, anything—"

"Whheee!" Two-year-old Ethan appeared, swinging an open bag of dried bean soup mix as he whirled in circles. A shower of beans rattled down on our hardwood entryway.

She ignored him, eyeing me grimly. "Let's talk about yesterday. You could have buckled down, gotten more done. Just what were you doing up there in the play fort with your boys?"

"Yesterday?" I stooped down to gather beans, grimacing as they dug into my knees. "Oh, it was the first day of spring. We needed to celebrate. We were having a little picnic of peanut butter sandwiches."

She closed her eyes in reproof. "And this morning? You could have gotten an earlier start on your work."

I wavered for a moment, then shook my head slowly. "I don't see how. I can't pass up my morning snuggle with Chandy. He won't do that forever, you know."

I thought for a second. "And then later, all three of us were crawling out of the sleeping bag, pretending to be caterpillars turning into butterflies."

Her lips pressed together in a thin line. "I see. You know, the zipper on that sleeping bag has needed repair for months." She hoisted her black book and began to scribble, pressing hard. "I'm going to have to write you up. These are called Vi-o-lations, missy. Violations of the work ethic. Infractions of the royal 'I've got to be all things to all people' code. Offenses against the order of the overloaded—"

"OK," I heard myself say. I sounded a lot braver than I felt.

"OK?" Her narrow eyes narrowed even more. "OK?"

I dug into my pocket and snatched out an eyebrow pencil. "I'm writing you up too then," I said. "On...on...this!" I bent and ripped a page from the Snow White coloring book lying on the floor.

She gave a snort of disbelief and said, "I don't think so!"

"Yes, I am," I rattled on. "And your penalty is...uh...that you have to sit in the sun on my back porch doing absolutely nothing."

Her hand flew to her throat.

"For 10 whole minutes."

She looked visibly shaken.

"And that's not all. You have to notice how beautiful the blossoms are on our hawthorn tree."

She grew pale.

"You have to see the squirrel hang by his tail and raid our bird feeder. You have to eat two of the chocolate bear cookies we made on Saturday. And then...," I delivered the coup de grâce. "You have to be kissed—messily, and smack on the lips—by a little boy who whispers, 'I love you berry, berry much.' "

"Why, I never!!" she spluttered, her face livid.

"Yes, I thought so," I said softly. "You never. You never do those things, do you? I used to be just like that, but I'm learning a better way."

She put her face up close to mine. "No, I'll tell you how you used to be. You used to produce, you used to achieve. Oh, it makes this stuff you're doing now look like...like child's play!"

She made one last desperate attempt. Grabbing my shoulders, she pleaded, "Okay, repeat this after me: Just-stay-on-task. Just-stay-on-task."

I tried to repeat it, I honestly did. But for some funny reason, instead of "Just stay on task," my words kept coming out, "Kids-grow-so-fast. Kids-grow-so-fast."

She stared at me like I was an alien life form. The last time I saw her she was practically running to her car.

I closed the door and hurried to the kitchen counter. I had something important to add to my to-do list. In careful letters I wrote: "Let go of guilt over never, ever getting done." Then with a big smile and a flourish, I crossed it off my list.

*If we have no privacy, we have no sacredness:
we lose our boundaries and have no place within
that is holy to ourselves. Take away our
sacredness, and we lose our core.* [1]

LEWIS SMEDES

❧

*Keep thou thy dreams—
the tissue of all wings is woven first of them.* [2]

VIRNA SHEARD

Chapter Five

Keep a Room of Your Own

I GUESS YOU MAY HAVE HEARD BY NOW THAT MONA IS FINALLY GETTING A ROOM OF HER OWN. MONA LISA, THAT IS. THE Louvre has decided that with all the people who want to see her, she needs and deserves a private gallery. So she's being rehung in her own tasteful room.

Personally, I think this may be why she has worn that enigmatic smile all these years. Maybe she knew that someday, somehow, the rest of the world would catch up with her and recognize what she has known all along: A lady needs her space.

I think of Mona in her private room and feel an odd sense of vindication for every mom who has ever locked herself in the bathroom and yelled through the door, "I'll be out sometime in the next century! Go ahead without me!"

Isn't it ironic the way life unfolds sometimes? During my single years I had plenty of physical space of my own, a little too much. My own apartment, my own car, my own table for one. There were days when my skin virtually ached for hugs or even a caring hand on my arm. It wasn't a passionate embrace I needed; it was simple human contact. I felt so touch-starved that even an accidental bump or brush up against a coworker in a crowded work aisle could set off waves of longing inside.

These days my waves of longing are of a different sort. Now I am the mom of two little boys who bounce out of bed each day like eager contestants in an extreme sport. Daily life is defined by great quantities of tumbling, crawling, climbing, wrestling, whooping, galloping, sliding and hiding. This very minute, my boys would love nothing better than to lie in wait around a corner, tackle me around the knees, and truss me up like a calf with a rope.

On some days I can be roped and rustled with the best of them. But on others, I envy Mona her room. I would love nothing better than to sit on a display shelf somewhere—a very high shelf—like an exquisite vase or priceless masterpiece, untouched by human hands. Not forever. Just for a while...maybe until I started to collect a little dust.

That brings to mind a poem I wrote when I was a teenager.

Oh, Lord, to have a separate shelf on which to humbly perch,
To have a hidden corner still where no one thinks to search.
To have a cozy little nook in which to crawl and hide,
A simple and a silent place with no one else inside.
To stop for just a moment now and let my whirlwind cease,
To have a precious separate shelf within a separate peace.

Isn't it something that in my first blush of womanhood— before pimples and a first date, and eons before babies, a Day-Timer, a mortgage or impending wrinkles—I instinctively knew I needed a place of my own. A hiding place, a hearing place, a hoping place with my name on the door.

I still do. I'm a little too tall now to hide in a tent made of bedsheets or to close myself into a big cardboard appliance box or crawl into the space under the basement steps like I did as a little girl. But a place of my own can be wherever I make it.

Susanna Wesley, the mom of John and Charles Wesley (and 18 other children!) knew that well. She supposedly would sit down and throw her big apron over her head just to create a private space of her own. Now that's the spirit! And I believe that's also the Spirit.

"Be still," invites the Lord, "and know that I am God."[3] Reading between the lines, I think I hear Him saying something like this to me: Find a room of your own and send yourself there. Not for punishment but for all the right reasons. Here are just a few:

- Because blessed is she who doesn't continually try to run on fumes.
- Because every mom who is so graced at giving, needs some time to take in, too.
- Because she who can magically create a robot out of foil and an oatmeal box; she who can create lunch out of leftover pasta, half a banana

and the last of the milk; she who can create an adventure out of getting the cracked windshield repaired needs a little time and space to be "re-created" herself.

- Because anyone who would tuck the world safely into bed at night—if only she could get her arms around everybody—needs to be cuddled by a few dreamy moments wrapped around her shoulders like a favorite comforter.

- Because a mom who so willingly kisses little faces needs to be assured she's not watching her own face disappear, rubbed out a little at a time, like yesterday's chalk drawings blurring on the front walk.

Oh, we don't mean to do that. We don't knowingly volunteer to begin to lose ourselves. But it can happen a little at a time. Life, especially life with small children, is wonderful and wild and full. All at once it can just seem that the last straw is perpetually around the next corner. Somewhere along the busy way we not only bump ourselves to the bottom of our mental list, we bump ourselves right off the list. And we hardly know it has happened. Our voices get a little shrill, our tempers run a little high, and it's all little wonder. That's it exactly: little wonder. We end up flat-souled and way too tired.

That must be where I was that afternoon I lined everyone up like a drill sergeant, demanding to know who was tracking chocolate all over our carpet. After a thorough check of every possible suspect, I discovered the guilty party. *Whoops.* Were those the sad remains of a chocolate chip clinging to the bottom of my sock? You've had those days, haven't you? Sometimes we just lose our sense of wonder and joy in what we're doing, and maybe even in who we are. Nobody needs to ask, "Are we having fun yet?" We know the answer.

ళ ళ ళ

I don't know about you, but for me, carving out solo time to regroup is harder than carving a frostbitten pumpkin with a popsicle stick. There are about a billion other things to do, at least half of them urgent. But look. Even if I was the Old Woman in the Shoe, with her unruly tribe of assorted kids, I'm sure I could somehow reclaim a half hour from every 24 hours just to get reacquainted with myself. So could you, couldn't you?

Granted, it takes some creativity and determination. But you're talking here to the woman who once heaved a maple dining room table over a banister and up two flights of steps because my friend and I decided it would look "so perfect" upstairs. It takes some trial and error, some new ways of thinking, to give time back to myself.

But like most women, if I'm convinced something is really worthwhile, I will move heaven and earth to help it happen.

So I'm not speaking in misty metaphors here. Do you have a room? With a door? That's the way to start. On a regular basis take your body to some sort of quiet place. Do not pass go. Do not plan tonight's dessert. Do not clip the cat's claws or gather up toy cars or vagabond crayons along the way. Just go. Just do it.

For me the room of choice is usually my bedroom. Once I am behind my closed door, this nurturer gives herself permission to become the nurturee. This means I say hello to myself again. I take a deep breath, gather my thoughts, slow my pulse and unjangle my nerves. I try to remember why I am doing what I am doing. I look at something beautiful to remind myself of Jesus, the Beautiful One.

"Sounds like work to me," you might be murmuring. Well, in a way it is. It's the work of learning to still and nourish your soul. That isn't just for monks, you know. It's for moms, too. Maybe especially for moms. "Certain springs are tapped only when we are alone," Anne Morrow Lindbergh observes. "The artist knows he must be alone to create; the writer, to work out his thoughts; the musician to compose; the saint, to pray. But women need solitude in order to find again the true essence of themselves."[4]

True essence. It sounds like the perfect name for an exotic cologne, but it doesn't come bottled, gift-boxed and priced by the quarter of an ounce. My experience has been that true essence is free and available exclusively through one Source. Who knows the true essence of me better than the God who created me? Although a room of my own is for me, it's also a place to offer Him more room in me. It's a place to find not only my true essence, but His. One of the ways I like to do this is by praying — talking all kinds of things over with Him.

Any woman who — like me — has lost her wedding ring at the mall and has tearfully found it again underneath a crammed rack of denim dresses has very few doubts about whether God hears and answers prayer. (But I still have one or two questions about how and when He answers!)

I find that my prayers come in assorted sizes and shapes — soft ones, questioning ones, promising ones, praising ones, sometimes pleading ones and once in a while even angry ones. In this season of my life, when simplicity is everything, my prayers are one predictable length: short. I try to remember that God sees the substance hidden in every sentence, every sigh, even in every silence of my "crazy-quilt" prayers. I may pray by the inch but I hope and believe by the mile.

"God, be a provider to those families in North Korea who are hungry and have so little."

"Please help me...my PMS is killing me this month."

"Be close to those teenagers who ran through the guardrail on our street last night."

"Help our government leaders to be people of integrity, Father. Influence them, draw them to want to follow Your ways."

"And Lord, could You help me come up with an easy way to teach Chandy how to tie his shoes?"

Simple prayers are like small hidden stitches that shape me and hold my life together. Talking with God is like a running thread that reminds me that even though I drop a lot of stitches in the intricate knitting of my life, Jesus is the One who keeps the whole thing from unraveling. Somehow He keeps His design emerging.

❧ ❧ ❧

"Heaven and earth will pass away," Jesus says, "but My words will by no means pass away."[5] Those are eternal words in a world where so much does pass away. And so quickly.

Ethan barrels by me and bangs his head on the edge of our kitchen counter. Wasn't it just yesterday that he could scamper underneath with room to spare? Alex comes home with the sad news that a coworker, a fairly young man, has died of cancer. Bulldozers, brawny and yellow and determined, circle a parcel of wooded land adjacent to our house and begin biting into the firs, flattening everything for a new housing development.

I sit with delicate cookies balanced on my lap, listening to a speaker at a women's meeting. Change is no longer incremental in our culture, she points out. Constant change has become a state of being.

Her words resonate inside me; the next day I am still thinking about them. It isn't my imagination that life holds still even less today than it used to. What lasts forever? How do I live with others in a way that matters forever? Where can I nest securely and not get swept away, even in a tsunami of changes?

Sometimes I feel like Noah's dove, circling, searching for a welcoming green branch above the high tides. "I am the same, yesterday, today and forever," Jesus says.[6] I wing in His direction by opening His Word. I read His stories, His truths that will always be true.

God has known and loved me from the very start—even before I did somersaults inside my mom—and He will love me forever.[7]

His love will never take me where His grace cannot keep me.[8]

I am not here by accident. I am here by God's appointment, in this nation, in this generation, in this family.[9]

Jesus brought heaven's best to me and I can turn around and bring it to those around me. I can make a lasting difference.[10]

God, who has started such a good work in me, is a Finisher.[11]

This world is not my home. Heaven is a real place where I will go on living and learning.[12]

No matter how fierce the battle gets, love wins. Always. Always. Always.[13]

I read even if it is often only a bite-sized portion—one verse, one chapter—because I want to feed my soul with eternity. There are times when the Bible is not an easy read for me. It takes more mental energy than I feel I have. I wonder how in the world these strange words apply to my life. I yawn. Sometimes it seems like nothing is happening inside me. Until later. Often much later. When the jeep coughs and dies. When Ethan cuts a hole in his new shirt. When I need wisdom or stamina or trust. Or just an extra four or five arms.

Oh, I don't always respond like a total saint. But neither am I just a survivor. Deep inside me there is an expanding little reservoir of purpose, patience, perspective that wasn't there before. I think that is called a quiet growth in grace and character. All may not always be right in the world. But my God is always in His heaven, working out His loving purposes for His glory and our good.[14] I know. I have reminded myself of this, stretched out on my bed with my Bible, in a room of my own.

◈ ◈ ◈

When I'm in a room of my own I also like to think of Pinky and emulate her. Pinky is the fluffy black-and-white hamster at Chandler's preschool. She has a very entertaining cage with all kinds of brightly colored plastic tunnels and a nice wheel to run on. But Pinky seems to prefer to nose around in her cedar chips, munch on a hamster treat or curl up serenely into a little ball for a nap.

Sometimes we put our faces close to the glass of her cage and tap on it, trying to coax Pinky toward her wheel. She sits motionless, blinking black button eyes at us, probably thinking, *The giant humans just don't seem to get it.* She knows there is a time to run the tunnels and wheel, but this is simply not the time. Pinky is one smart little hamster. Her down time is inviolate.

Pinky helps inspire me toward the happy art of "putzing," or puttering around. Sometimes this involves my sock drawer. In the privacy of a room of my own, I pull that drawer out and completely reorganize it. I reunite all the estranged socks with their partners, stand them up neatly in rows and step back, surveying the results with a smile. I have achieved the impossible: I have actually finished a task I started. Suddenly, order reigns in the cosmos.

Sometimes I also nibble on something I really enjoy, like jelly beans—the kind that come in a million or so assorted flavors. I don't know if you've noticed, but there are "recipes" on some of the jelly bean packages. If you eat certain beans together, say chocolate, banana and cherry, the combination is supposed to taste exactly like a banana split. I dig through all those beans to unearth the right ones and try it out. Activities like this do very little to expand my mind, but strangely, they do wonders for my soul. Sometimes I burn a scented candle and actually notice the fragrance. Or turn on music and really listen. Or read poetry, the nonheadache-producing kind that is easy to grasp.

Often I read a book, skipping around wherever I want to. Believe it or not, the Book Police have never once issued me a citation. Sometimes I flip through magazines and imagine myself actually whipping up that roast pheasant with chili pesto and cornbread stuffing. I envision myself placing a tasteful bowl of gold-leafed fruit in the center of my table for the holidays à la Martha Stewart. Or swirling around in that strapless velvet dress, swinging a very tiny purse (with no room for wet wipes), my eyes bright, my lipstick perfect, my earrings matched. I remind myself that, yes, that day will come.

I ponder whether there is anything to what I have heard—that the secret to a successful life is finding a good hairstyle and sticking with it. Sometimes I blow up my bath pillow and sink down into a hot tub up to my chin, keeping a wasteful trickle of warm water running on my extended toes. While my mirror fogs and every tense muscle relaxes, I consider this: The power of a good, long soak and a fluffy towel is just impossible to overestimate.

I often write "postcards" to myself just to stay in touch. I use regular three-by-five index cards. I never mail them, of course. I just keep them in a rubber-banded stack on my nightstand. I started doing this when Ethan was about a year old, when it so distressed me that I couldn't remember what day it was, let alone ponder anything that was happening in my life. So many feelings and experiences, so little time.

At the top of each card I write the date (and sometimes the previous day's weather) and immediately feel oriented. Then I just jot down notes to myself about what is happening in my private world. Baby milestones. What I'm sad, glad or mad about. What I hope for, dread or simply can't figure out. Whatever is important to me. The size of the card helps me keep it short. I don't worry if I miss some days; I'll get back to it. I have done this for almost two years now and I never have to write at the bottom of one of the postcards, "Having a great time. Wish you were here." I *am* here, in tune with my own life.

෧෧ ෧෧ ෧෧

A room of my own has also been a place of unexpected discovery. There is no need to notify our tax assessors, but it was in my room that I first realized that our home is sitting on view property. We have a three-by-six-foot bedroom window that opens to a view of our very typical suburban cul-de-sac: front doors, driveways, kids' bikes, mailboxes. But if I pull our venetian blinds all the way to the top and lie on my back on the bed, our window frames a gorgeous sweep of sky and clouds and the tops of the giant firs across the street. Sometimes I lie down and do nothing but watch the fingers of the tree tops bending and swaying in the breeze.

It isn't easy. I am often uneasy with my insistence on making activity secondary in a room of my own. It seems risky, reckless, like stacking the apples on top of the eggs in the grocery cart or leaving a preschooler and an indelible inkpad alone in a room together. I keep coaching myself along the way: *T-shirts are not shrinking in the dryer, relationships are not dying on the vine, and planets are not colliding because you are not at the helm for the next 30 minutes.* I say these things to myself even as guilt whines in my ear like a dentist's drill. Doing things like lying down must wait until everything is done.

 *A woman who keeps a sensible piece of herself to herself finds peace to give away to her world.*

On good days I swallow hard and pull guilt's plug, saying to myself, *Everything else is never done, so these few minutes are mine.* (Right?) One thing is for sure. Learning to keep a room of my own hasn't been a Saturday project. It takes time and persistence. But do you know what I think I'm beginning to see? That a woman who keeps a sensible piece of herself to herself finds peace to give away to her world.

🍀 🍀 🍀

I heard a story once about a man lacking peace who was looking at redwood trees, not firs like the ones outside our bedroom window. He was a classic type A tourist on a guided tour to see those majestic California giants. Before long, his nonstop activity and endless barrage of questions had the rest of the group ready to wring his neck. At one point he turned to the guide and blurted out, "Okay, okay, now how did you say these trees get to be this size?"

The guide was silent for a moment, then said pointedly, "I think they just stood still and grew tall." There. That is what I'm discovering in a room of my own. I can stand still and grow tall.

Part of growing tall is dreaming. "Within your heart," counsels Louise Driscoll, "keep one still secret spot where dreams may go."[15] Do you have a place like that? Because you need it. Me, too.

For a while my place for dreams was our Dodge Caravan. I just didn't know it. During the boys' infant years our van was a mobile "room of my own," but only after it did the impossible as a soothing nanny, rocking Chandler and Ethan simultaneously to sleep for at least 45 minutes. I can still remember peeking hopefully into the rearview mirror and seeing to my elation that their heads were bobbing, their little chins hitting their chests on each new bump in the road. I would pull smoothly into the nearest McDonalds, take a deep breath, buy a Diet Coke and a newspaper and sit and read.

Oh, this was heaven! Those wonderful, humble rest stops revived in me a long-neglected love for words and reading, which led me back to a love for writing. Which led, eventually, to this book. I just wonder if it all would have happened without a room of my own. And so I plan to keep right on visiting my hiding, hearing, hoping place until coming to the quietness becomes my habit, a wonderful little rut. And then I'll keep in mind what Erma Bombeck said: "Not every rut needs fixing."[16]

Oh, my slice of time alone has certainly not been the magic solution to everything. I still can't load the kids into the van faster than a speeding bullet or leap over tall agendas at a single bound. But I can do something even better. I can laugh more easily. Live more lightly. Enjoy things just as they are a little more often. I can remember that there is a whole lot more to this mommy than mere movement. I can even dare to believe—one nap, one prayer, one pause at a time—that I really don't have to earn love by proving my usefulness.

I know that each time I send myself to my room, little eyes are watching me and drawing big conclusions . Maybe Chandler and Ethan can just grow up knowing the truth that ease is a holy art to be learned and that quiet time and play, naps and wonder are for big people, too. I hope it becomes as natural as breathing to them to care for and water the gardens of their own souls.

As for Mona Lisa, we might know a lot more about her if Michelangelo had done a full-length portrait. Personally, I think she was "eating up" her chance to pose—to sit there like a lump for a few blissful hours while a friend watched her kids. My guess is that Mona was wearing her favorite bunny slippers under that robe and had her hands crossed so carefully because her manicure was still tacky to the touch. Maybe she even had a bowl of popcorn within reach just in case the munchies hit her. Wise woman.

Someday I might just have to hop on a plane and go visit her in that new private gallery in the Louvre. *Hmmm.* Well, for now I can at least spread out a few maps, draw a red circle around Paris, even nibble on a petit four or two. And dream...later...in a room of my own.

Because I Love a Good Story...

The angel was very short and very eager to learn. He had a small halo and a big clipboard. His new assignment involved women and he was intent on learning all he could about them.

"Let's begin," said the tall angel.

In an instant they were at a café, observing two women seated together over coffee at a small, round table.

"Tell me what they're doing," the tall angel said.

At just that moment, one of the women laughed, put her hand on her friend's arm and leaned forward to say something.

"They're just talking," replied the short angel.

"Wrong. They're having a Good Talk. That's different. Just talking happens all the time and often accomplishes nothing. But a Good Talk like this is the air a woman breathes. A Good Talk can keep love alive, turn winter to spring, change the course of lives, keep lives on course. A Good Talk can change everything, even though nothing has changed."

"I see...," said the short angel, with a puzzled frown. He scribbled a note on his clipboard.

The tall angel handed him a silver key on a purple cord. "Here," he said, "open the trunk and you'll learn more."

The short angel eased open the lid of the ornately carved chest.

"The Master gathers impossibilities in this trunk and works on them," explained the tall angel, resting one glowing hand on the open lid. "These are things for which there is no earthly hope. The desperately sick child, the loveless marriage, the long-cherished but unfulfilled dream, the broken heart, the unchanged life, the godless nation."

He shook his head in wonder. "Women work so well with the Master on these because they don't know when to give up. They can hope beyond all hope."

He looked closely at the short angel. "If there are things for which you dream," he advised, "find a woman to hope with. They do it so beautifully."

The short angel did have a secret dream or two in his heart. But before he could say a word he found himself in a room full of beautiful glass bottles. They lined the large room from floor to ceiling, shining in every imaginable color and shape.

"Don't tell me!" he cried. "I think I know where we are now. The psalmist David said to the Lord, 'You have kept all my tears in Your bottle.' Is this the great room where those bottles are kept?"

"Look closely," urged the tall angel.

The short angel stepped forward to examine one bottle, then another. He turned to his mentor, brow furrowed, and said, "Why, these are empty."

"No, they're full. They are full of tears never cried, because a woman was there. These are the reminders of loving acts that often go unseen and unheralded—the hug offered at just the right time, the everyday task done with such care, the comforting word, the soft shoulder, the smile of encouragement that says 'I believe in you.' I shudder to think of the world without a woman's tenderness."

"The world is very dark and dangerous," observed the short angel. "And a woman seems so...so delicate that

I wonder if she can hold up very well at all."

"Ah, the world is not what it once was," agreed the tall angel, stroking his chin. "And a woman needs a good deal of love and care to face its perils. But the world also has great hopes and new beginnings, lullabies and loveliness. And a woman is at her best when she is discovering them. Or creating them."

"But she's so soft," said the short angel, a note of doubt in his voice. "Like a summer breeze or a rose petal, or... or...."

"Or the fur of a lioness?" offered the tall angel. "Have you pulled duty in the birthing rooms yet? Have you ever seen a woman in action that way?"

The short angel's face reddened and he stared at his shoes. "No, not just yet."

"Then have you ever been a comforter at the Harbor of Good-byes?"

The short angel shook his head again.

"The wind is so biting at the Harbor," continued the tall angel, "and the blackness so complete that even men try to stay away sometimes. But the women...the women almost always come. They seem to know how to lean into the wind and wait for the light."

The short angel was quiet as his teacher slipped an arm around his shoulder and said, "Just one last thing for today. Come and see one of the most beautiful and powerful sights in all the world."

As soon as these words were spoken the short angel found himself perched on little Andrew Murray's bed, dangling his celestial feet over the edge.

"Here it is," said the tall angel in a hushed tone. He pointed to a rumpled spot on the worn quilt, right beside seven-year-old Andrew's baseball mitt.

The short angel studied the rumpled spot closely. "Here *what* is?" he whispered back. "*This* is one of the most beautiful and powerful sights in all the world? It looks more like a place where the cat has been curled up."

The tall angel smiled. "I know. Would you ever guess that kings and wise men are made here, legacies are given, love is proved and all heaven moves? You see, this is where Andrew's mom kneels to pray for him. This spot is the print of her elbows on the bed."

Suddenly, a thunderous roar echoed all around them. "What is that?" cried the short angel, clutching the edge of the bed, his lips quivering. "A catastrophic earthquake? The end of the age?"

The tall angel stood a bit taller, a solemn look on his face. "No," he replied. "That is the sound of furniture being arranged and rearranged and rearranged again all over the world."

The short angel's face was a study of perplexity and wonder. "Woman?" he said weakly, already guessing the answer. "I guess I still have a lot to learn."

The tall angel just winked.

❧

Pictures the Spirit has already taken:
All of us standing, undaunted, unshaken,
Mother and father, children and friends
Smiling into our Father's wide lens.

Tucked in the pages of His book of life,
Brother and sister, husband and wife.
Precious and simple and glowing like gold,
His family portrait that never grows old.

DEENA LEE WILSON

Chapter Six

*Live Beyond
the Cover and
Title Page*

MOMMY, WHAT DOES A MARMOSET EAT?" CHANDY ASKED ME AT THE DINNER TABLE.

I paused, a forkful of chopped steak en route to my mouth. Do you think I could come up with even a wild guess about what a marmoset orders for dinner? No. I was having a hard enough time just trying to bring up a mental picture of how a marmoset looks. Is it like a cat? An anteater? A monkey?

I heard Chandler answering his own question. "He eats gooey white stuff."

I lifted one eyebrow in interest. "Really? You mean...larvae?"

"Uh-huh. That's it." Chandler waved his spoon affirmatively. "Larvae."

I started to fork up some rice then gently laid my fork back down.

"Syrup is made of that," Chandler went on. He was quite the wellspring of information. "Made of larvae."

Several thoughts flashed through my mind. One was that I am the mother of boys, which explains why we were discussing marmoset feeding habits at the dinner table. Another mental flash was that my son actually believed I habitually poured liquefied larvae onto his morning pancakes. Another thought was that he might very well be college age before the veil lifted and he discovered the truth, because I was just going to eat my dinner and let this one slide.

Alex pursed his lips doubtfully. "Syrup from larvae? I think you might have some things mixed up a little."

"Papa!" Chandler huffed. "Someone around here knows a whole lot more than you think!"

Yes, well. It does take some living for all these odd beliefs we acquire to be debunked, doesn't it? I only know because I spent about the first 15 years of my life thinking it was just fascinating that an olive grows with that little red flap of a tongue stuffed inside the hole. The autonomy of pimentos came as a total shock to me. The final indignity was the searing realization that everyone else on this planet except me had probably always known about it.

I've found that it's easy to amass quite a collection of misinformation while moving through life, some of it funny, some not. Ideas like the belief that life should always be fair; that loving should be natural and easy, not labored over and learned; that the lightning bolt of loss only strikes other people's lives, not mine. And surely not twice in the same place. Isn't there some kind of law about that?

I thought about that again one morning as I diapered Ethan on the bed in the nursery. I knew it wouldn't be long before the baby motif of the room most likely would give way to a little-boy decor—bright airplanes or cowboys or balls and bats. But not yet. For now, the nursery is still pastels—soft blues and greens and yellows. A parade of plump, amiable bunnies with floppy ears tumbles around the top of the room in a wide border.

Chandler's bed sits against one blue-striped wall, and on that wall is a decoration—a cluster of cloth balloons, each one about the size of a dinner plate. Each balloon is a different soft color with a piece of cord dangling down for its string.

Two of the balloons—a blue and green one—appear to be free spirits. They float a little farther away and higher than the others, as if at any moment they might playfully pull away and rise together up the wall, right through the nursery ceiling and into the sky above our house. Except...their cords are still entwined with the others.

I hung those two balloons that way on purpose. I remember balancing on Chandler's bed one day and reaching up to carefully knot the cords together. That is a small thing, I know. But small, healing, hopeful reminders can go a very long way when lightning strikes. Especially when there are none of the usual things to help with the momentum of good-bye—no funeral, no pictures, no lock of hair, so few keepsakes.

You see, there are two babies, Amanda and Kiley, whom we did not get to know or keep. We never got a chance to cuddle them, count their pudgy toes, or debate about whose ears or eyes they had. They unexpectedly flew high, bypassing our hugs and hopes for them. They left our lives almost as quickly as they came, but they have never left our hearts. In spite of all that happened, they will always be ours. There is a very long cord, a hope and a reality, that still anchors them to us. And that has made all the difference.

Few things about babies unfolded for us in exactly the way Alex and I had expected they would. When I look back, the exact chronology of all the surprises blurs a little. But neither of us expected to marry later in life, in our thirties. And then we didn't expect the waiting. (Wasn't starting a family supposed to be as easy as falling off a log?) We didn't expect to not be expecting, but we kept praying. We didn't expect the monthly roller coaster of hope and disappointment. Or eventually, the specialist. Or basal temperature readings ad nauseam. And more waiting. We didn't expect all the questions, the rising concerns, the thin edge of panic. We didn't expect the tests, the endometriosis, the surgery. More prayers, more waiting.

There was obviously a colossal mistake somewhere. Someone had handed us the wrong script and we were navigating numbly through it, scrambling our lines and missing our cues. We knew God was with us; we knew that He loved us. But this was not the story line we had imagined. Couldn't God see that part of our cast was missing? Our family life was supposed to include a family. Tummies to tickle and toys to trip over, lullabies and loose teeth, the wonder years and the endless whys. Instead we were the ones asking the endless questions, trying hard to trust.

Maybe it was because of all the detours and delayed dreams along the way that each pregnancy was such a marvel to us. I still remember that Easter morning, that innocent, unrepeatable, almost unbelievable first time. We excitedly strapped our camera to a backyard fence post and snapped an automatic picture of ourselves in our Sunday best, hugging under the big hawthorn tree in the uncertain light of a spring morning. It was Resurrection Day, the perfect day to discover the perfect secret: A new life had wondrously begun in me. Could we dare to believe it? Finally, finally, finally. A baby! It was as if the interrupted joyful music of our lives started playing our song again. We were really going to be a mom and dad.

"Miscarriage" was just never a word in our vocabulary until abruptly and dreadfully it was. I didn't want to own it; I didn't want to know that word, ever. No more than I wanted to know, with an awful and deep intuitiveness, what the bleeding meant or what it meant when the technician tipped the ultrasound screen away from me and said in a careful tone, "We need to have your doctor talk to you now." Suddenly it wasn't just the ultrasound screen tipping; it was my whole world—my faith, my future—upending in the icy waters of reality. There was no mistake, no miracle and no heartbeat. This happened to other people, not to us. Oh, please God, not to us. *Baby, come back...we love you.*

When you long for a baby as we did, and you find that one is finally coming to you, and then suddenly, inexplicably, it isn't, it feels like the worst of broken promises, the end of the world. And it is the end of the world as you dreamed and hoped it to be. Whether it is your first baby or your fifth doesn't matter. What matters is that the real little person, the priceless gift you were poised to receive, is not coming after all. Not in six months. Not by Christmas. Not ever.

How could there suddenly be no need for us to decorate a nursery? How could I be a mommy-to-be one day and the next day just be me again? How could I box away the little fine-tooth comb, the yellow rattle, the pink pillow to hang on the nursery doorknob with the embroidered caution, "Shhh...Baby Sleeping"? Where was there a box big enough for the pieces of my dreams and hopes? How could the iron grip of grief make my whole body ache like the worst flu of my life? Why our baby, who was so wanted? Why, when we had tried so hard, prayed so much, waited so long?

Tell me, how can the end of a life so tiny be such a titanic loss? It boggles the mind. The grief of losing Amanda and Kiley was like being jerked upside down by my ankles and left to hang, dumbfounded and paralyzed, as the right-side-up world paraded by me as usual. How could other people just go on living as they always did—fixing noodle casseroles for dinner, fussing about the weather, celebrating birthdays and Mother's Day, getting their tires rotated and their checkbooks balanced—when our babies were gone, when "normal" had disappeared for us?

I couldn't right myself, no matter how hard I tried. Now I know that no one really can. Sorrow is finished when it's finished and not one nanosecond sooner. If you've been there, you know that, too. It is a long time before you can really whisper good-bye, isn't it? And even then you have to say it so many times.

"When grief picks us up," writes Paula D'Arcy, "it never puts us down in the same spot. We move. We change. We are all that we were before, plus the experience which has hurt us, plus the new individual who emerges to cope, and to move on."[1] It took a long time, but when grief finally did set me down, I began to see that though Amanda and Kiley's lives were almost too short to be calendared, their lives were not small. They left me, their mom, a lasting legacy. They never looked into my eyes and yet they helped me see. They never had the chance to know me, but they changed me forever. They never even touched me, but through them I touched one of my deepest fears and found that God was deeper.

❧ ❧ ❧

"Cobweb," Ethan said softly as our family stood on the fenced boardwalk drinking in the view.

Spread out before us were acres and acres of protected wetlands and wildlife. It was a haven full of rushes, cattails and wildflowers. It bustled with bugs, birds and other small creatures.

"Look, Ethie!" I enthused, all ready to give an impromptu nature lesson. "What do you see?"

"Cobweb." That was the reply that rose from around my knees, from somewhere under the pointed green hood of his sweatshirt.

Cobweb? It took me back for a minute. A pond, yes. Big birds, yes. Lots of blue sky, right. But cobweb? I knelt down next to him and immediately I understood. He was standing next to the wooden railing. Stretched right at his eye level, from post to post, was the shimmering work of one very industrious spider. It was all Ethan could see. He didn't have a clue about my view beyond those posts. He saw only what his little nose was almost touching—a delicate spinning of circles that would probably be swept away by the next strong wind.

Sometimes I'm just like Ethan—too short and too small to see the long view beyond the circles of daily projects and pursuits right in front of me. God used Amanda and Kiley to lift me above the cobwebs, to help me remember to look up and beyond this life.

Do you believe in heaven? I do. It isn't a new belief for me. For almost as long as I can remember, even as a child, I have known that heaven is real. But heaven was a faraway place for someday—scattered lights winking on a distant misty shore. It was comfortingly there, but it was not close or soon.

I can honestly say I didn't fully know what a treasure I had in heaven until I didn't have my babies anymore. C. S. Lewis suggests,

> You never know how much you really believe anything, until its truth or falsehood becomes a matter of life and death to you. It is easy to say you believe a rope to be strong and sound as long as you are merely using it to cord a box. But suppose

you had to hang by that rope over a precipice. Wouldn't you then first discover how much you really trusted it?... Only a real risk tests the reality of a belief.[2]

When tragedy, especially your first personal encounter with death, unties and upends all your neat boxes, you must discover or rediscover what is real.

I didn't dream all that heaven meant to me until it meant that my babies still exist. They were so imperfect, so unfinished, so fragile. Some would say that in all their tininess they were not people at all. They were wads of tissue and bone, underdeveloped cells, potential life in the rough. They were perhaps somethings, but neither of them was a distinctive someone. It was too soon. Yes, their leaving was far too soon for me. But I believe it was not too soon for them to fully be.

When I open my Bible in a search for substance, not sentiment, I clearly hear a heartbeat. Shhh. Listen with me to Psalm 139:15,16, *NKJV*:

> *My frame was not hidden from You,*
> *When I was made in secret,*
> *And skillfully wrought in the lowest*
> *parts of the earth.*
> *Your eyes saw my substance,*

being yet unformed.
And in Your book they all were written,
The days fashioned for me,
When as yet there were none of them.

Jeremiah 1:5 and Luke 1:39-43 echo with the same reassurance. Do you know what these passages say to me? That there's a whole lot more to us than skin and blood and bones. From that first spark of conception, you were you, and I was me, even though our physical bodies were still barely off the drawing board. Our personhoods—our souls and spirits—didn't sit around on suitcases, waiting to make sure all our rooms got finished before moving in. We were valid, meaningful people from that initial uniting of cells, the first brick, the letter *A.* We were us the whole time God was building our houses around us in the womb. We weren't physically durable, we weren't all that we would someday be, but we were truly present for God to know and love. That's not a small thought. But then, God isn't a small God. Only He could wrap so immense a treasure as life in such a tiny gift box.

And here is another wonderful truth that continues to comfort me, the mom who believes the 11th commandment surely must be, "Thou shalt hold hands and stay together." Amanda and Kiley are not lost. They are not floating somewhere, abandoned and afraid, in a dark void of nothingness. They are not disembodied or in limbo or oblivion. They are not reincarnated or somehow recycled into the essence of the wind and flowers and trees. My babies are simply and safely at home with Jesus in heaven. As small as they were, they had a destiny and a clear destination.

Do you know what this means to me? It means that I can sleep at night. It means I can let faith win out over fear. I can hold hope sure. I can heal. It was incredibly hard to say good-bye. But because Jesus has opened heaven for me, I didn't have to try to say an agonizing, "Good-bye forever." Instead I whispered through tears, "Good-bye for now."

It all comes down to this golden promise: I will see my babies someday. I know there will be at least two eager faces at the windows of heaven, watching for me. I'll tell you what I'm going to do. I'm not going to knock or ring the bell or wipe my feet or give a second thought to how my hair looks. I'm going to put my hand on the doorknob of heaven and tumble right in, laughing, because a precious part of me is already there. I'm going to find those babies and hold them so tight they can't breathe and they start begging for me to let them go. Finally, we will have that lost time for togetherness, the real conversations, the shared moments we couldn't have here. As glorious as that will be, it will be only a very small part of heaven's joys. I can't imagine how all that is even possible. It eludes my understanding, but it anchors my soul.

*Life in this world is just
the cover and title page; heaven is
Chapter One.*

For me it changes everything to remember that life doesn't begin in a delivery room and it doesn't end on the edge of a grave. Life is a glorious continuum, a never-ending story for Amanda and Kiley, for me, for every one of us. I don't walk around thinking about this every day, but I am an eternal creation and so are you. I will always be me; you will always be you. Permanently. We were designed to nestle close to our loving Creator and Savior. Forever. This world is not our home; heaven is home. Those are giant realities for me to try to get my heart around. C. S. Lewis helps me.

In his story, *The Last Battle,* he envisions what it will be like for us to step into heaven, into eternity.

> All of you are...dead. The term is over: the holidays have begun. The dream is ended: this is the

morning.... The things that began to happen after that were so great and beautiful that I cannot write them.... We can most truly say that they all lived happily ever after. But for them it was only the beginning of the real story. All their life in this world and all their adventures...had been only the cover and the title page: now at last they were beginning Chapter One of the Great Story, which no one on earth has read: which goes on forever, in which every chapter is better than the one before.[3]

Oh, how I love that image. Life in this world is just the cover and title page of my book, only the start of my unique, endless story. Heaven is Chapter One.

Chandler, who at five years old is even more at the beginning of his story than I am mine, knows a few things about heaven. Heaven is the place you get to go when you're "really old." I asked him once how old he thought really old was. I was curious since I knew that numbers and counting—especially up high—were still a little nebulous for him. *Really old,* by Chandler's confident estimation, must be "about eighteen-seventy-heaven-five" years old. Well, I think he has the right idea, putting heaven smack in the middle of things. Chandler knows heaven is where Jesus lives, where we will really see and touch Him. It is where you get a new body that never has any owies like "head eggs," and you can do cool things like walking right through walls. Heaven is where you don't cry anymore. Heaven is where Grandpa and Grandma Wilson live. Heaven is where the whole family gets to be together again. When I think about it, Chandler has a pretty good grasp of why home and hope is spelled h-e-a-v-e-n.

Ethan, of course, can't spell anything just yet. But if he could understand Lewis's view of our lives as an unfolding story, he would be the first to enthusiastically approve of it, as he does all things bookish.

Ethan was born enraptured by books—big, thick storybooks, catalogs, home schooling magazines. We used to peek into the nursery when he was tiny and see him lying there in his white crib on his belly, poring over the pages. "What do you think he's doing?" I would whisper to Alex. "What do you suppose he sees?" We knew that the letters and words were hieroglyphics to him, a locked world, but still he stared at them in fascination. He wasn't reading; he was somehow absorbing it all: the lines and loops of the letters, the feel of the pages, the colors and shapes of the pictures. I think my enduring memory of Ethan as a little boy will be him toddling contentedly around our house after me, an ever-present book tucked under his chubby arm.

As I watch Ethan and Chandler grow, it humbles me to think that in a sense they both will always carry me under one arm, close to their hearts. What they don't yet fully understand they are absorbing day by ordinary day: my lines and loops, the feel of my person and passions, the colors and shapes of my deepest beliefs and reasons for hope in God. "You are not only making memories," writes Valerie Bell, "you are the memories. In a deep, subconscious, unarticulated place, a parent stays with his or her child...forever."[4]

Forever? Forever is a really long time, isn't it? It sounds just right to me.

Because I Love a Good Story...

This summer Chandler was just the right age to be a ring-bearer for the first time, and he was summoned into service for two much-anticipated weddings.

"I'm going to be a ringbear?" He frowned dubiously, unsure whether this strange assignment was privilege or punishment. It took a little bit of explaining.

The first wedding was for a family friend. It was lovely and personal. It was a white steeple, stained glass, a horse-drawn carriage.

On the wedding morning, our family huddled together in a basement dressing room to be part of Chandler's transformation. Before we could say "cummerbund," he had peeled off his jeans, T-shirt, shoes and socks. He looked stricken and vulnerable when he turned around and realized that Alex was still struggling to separate the union of the hanger and the miniature white tuxedo.

"Papa!" he cried, "You gotta help me! Don't leave me like this!" All our emotions were running a little high that day.

In the end it was a guy kind of thing. Father and son worked as a team, heads together, to get "Ringbear" snapped, strapped and buttoned into his formalwear. (I think there were some gears and duct tape involved, too.) Finally it was time for the ceremonial final touch: Alex encased Chandy's little feet in those indestructible white plastic shoes and straightened his bow tie. I took one look and swallowed hard. Ringbear looked like he belonged on top of the wedding cake.

The wedding itself went off without a hitch...almost. I positioned myself toward the front of the church so I could coach Chandler down the aisle if he needed me. As family and friends filled the sanctuary, Ethan solemnly rose and filled his diaper. This was not a problem, though, since it guaranteed us plenty of pew space. We needed that extra room for all the snacks, toys and books we had carted along. We had enough supplies to provision a small army through a lean winter.

When the ceremony began, Chandler needed little coaching. With a reassuring send-off from Papa at the back of the church, he came stepping down the carpeted aisle on cue. He was carrying a big Bible with the ring glittering on a satin ribbon. He carried that Bible as reverently as if he was carrying the keys to a kingdom. (He was.)

Once at the front, he turned and assumed his position with the groomsmen as smoothly as if he had rehearsed at West Point. I'm sure it helped that Chandler had finger painted, hopped and danced, made chocolate chip cookies and splashed in our sprinkler with the bride. She just looked all dressed up like a fancy lady today. He knew who she really was beneath the pearls and lace; she was Coral, his baby-sitter and friend.

Two weeks later, the wedding was for Scott, Alex's handsome nephew. Scott had lit the candles at our wedding nine years ago. Now Michelle had lit his life. The wedding was classic and elegant. It was white pillars and arches, trailing ivy and a limo. Before it began, I chatted with family while Chandler lounged around with Scott and the "big boy" groomsmen. I smiled as I watched him closely watching them. He was clutching a scuba-diver action figure in one hand, a yellow plastic toy from a fast-food place in the other. He was Scott's twin; their black tuxes had been chosen to match.

When the ceremony began, the family was shoulder-to-shoulder in the pew. Ethan played musical laps on Alex and me. He looked darling in striped blue and white linen shorts, blue suspenders, a red polo shirt. The shorts would be too tight by the time he ate one mint at the reception, but there was no larger size, so I had bought them anyway. After all, how many times would Scott be getting married?

I tried to twist in the pew so I would have a clear view of everyone coming down the aisle. I felt the Velcro closure on the diaper bag grab something. When I yanked, I discovered that Ethan's cute white knee-highs were rapidly unraveling. I made a silent promise that from that day on I was going to be the only one in the family wearing hose.

Chandler marched down the aisle like a pro, this time carrying the ring on a pillow. He was balancing it like it was Cinderella's glass slipper. At the front, he turned, then stood rooted in place in front of the groomsmen, the top of his head just about at their waists.

"Bend your knees," I mouthed silently. I didn't want to be a hover-mom, but maybe I needed to be prepared to vault out of the pew just in case Chandler toppled like a sapling in a high wind. He didn't.

The ceremony was under way and my eyes grew misty. I dabbed at them, and it was just about then that I decided it wasn't such a good idea having Scott and

Chandler dressed in matching tuxedos. Because I blinked and suddenly it was Chandler, not Scott, who was the groom. He had found someone to give that glass slipper to. I blinked again and it was not Michelle looking luminous in her gown and veil, it was that little girl we had met at the park when Chandler was three.

I will never forget it. It was one of those rare days when everything felt so right in my world. I had renewed my driver's license and actually liked the photo. I had stepped on the scales and discovered I was two pounds lighter. Ethan was round and adorable at seven months and here we were at the park, my boys and I, on a warm, cloudless day. Chandler looked like the little prince of summer, tan and in perpetual motion, in a red T-shirt and jeans shorts. There was nothing I had to do; nowhere I had to be; nothing more I wanted. The sun was on my face and I was in heaven.

Chandler broke into my reverie. "Mommy!" He was yanking on my pants leg and he had someone in tow. "Look! I got a girl!" She could have been his sister, standing there willowy and winsome, with blue eyes and long blonde locks. Suddenly the two of them looked dangerously like a matched set.

My heart skipped a beat. My mouth went dry. My mind whirled ahead to a future day, so far away, so soon. "Mommy, I got a girl!"

Yipes! Was that a tear I was blinking back? I caught myself and bent down to give a friendly mommy smile and say "Hi" to this little playmate. But she—no, they—were already gone. Isn't that just the way it happens? As I straightened, I spotted them happily running off together, hand in hand.

I blinked again and Scott and Michelle, hand in hand, were back in their rightful places as bride and groom. And Chandler had not budged from his. He was doing so well today...almost too well. It seemed to me he was being a little too grown-up, a tad too perfect. But then, just when I was starting to get a bit wistful and worried, something wonderful began to happen right before my eyes.

Chandler started to fidget. He began twisting his feet, standing on the sides of those uncomfortable plastic shoes. My eyes brightened. He rolled his shoulders, started looking around. My heart lifted. Then he tipped his head slowly back and gave an eyeball-rolling, tonsil-revealing yawn. I broke into a smile. Scott and Michelle's big kiss was coming and so was the end of Ringbear's endurance. Another minute and the music soared and everyone began marching joyfully up the aisle.

Chandy came tumbling up the aisle with an eager look that shouted, "Where's the cake?!" His shirttail hung out on one side like a crumpled banner. His limp boutonniere clung to his lapel like a gasping survivor. He looked messy and rumpled and ready to play. He looked *wonderful.*

I wanted to stand up and cheer, "That's my boy!" My boy. For now. He is 5, not 15 or 25. I still have some years—unforgettable years—before he's the one in the big tux, giving the glass slipper and his heart away.

Until then, Chandler and Ethan, Alex and I have lots of living to do, places to go, people to see. We have a lot of "shade trees" of caring to plant. We have stories to live, to tell and to treasure, including God's greatest story of love. We have a lifetime of learn-as-you-go small beginnings to celebrate: first lost tooth, first grade, first bike, first sleepover, first job, first date, first love. New worlds are awaiting us.

We don't have any guarantees of forever here, but we will say yes to the irreplaceable gift of today. We will keep discovering that time for quietness is good, that stillness can be our rich soil for growing tall. We will keep helping each other look up, beyond the cobwebs, knowing that as precious as this life is, there is more good than we can dream of waiting for us with Jesus in heaven.

Someday we are going to do another wedding, the Really Big One. The invitations have gone out, but the R.S.V.P.s are still coming in. This wedding will be intimate and universal. It will be white robes and clean consciences, the best of the wine and the best of kept promises. Like Chandler in his tux, we're going to be transformed. We will be decked out in the love we can never quite seem to get enough of here. We're finally going to be wearing "forever" like it was made for us.

Although the turnout for the wedding will be huge, there will be something warmly familiar about every face. We will all clear our throats and sing new songs to our Lord together for the very first time. Then maybe we will all get choked up and pass around boxes of double tissue and cry tears for the very last time.

When the ceremony begins, I don't know if we will see any Ringbears. But we will see Jesus. And seeing Him, everything will make sense. Seeing Him, we will finally see things as they really are. I hope it won't catch us by surprise to see that it is the giving life that sparkles like an undying star, even more radiantly than the "gifted" life, and that the love that leads to giving has, like grace, always been free for the taking. I hope we'll be able to wink and whisper, "I knew that," when it becomes as clear as a cloudless morning that the small, steady, sometimes silly-looking pushes of day-by-day living and loving for Jesus are the real heroics of heaven.

That is so good for me to remember because I just have the funniest feeling that I may not be needing that

Academy Awards acceptance speech I practiced so many times in front of our hallway mirror when I was a teenager. I may never see my name go up in lights, but I sure hope I will always see my husband's eyes light up when I enter the room.

I may never have a velvet voice that soars where the air is thin or any big hits that promise to go platinum. But I sure hope that when my hair goes platinum, my boys will still remember me singing hits like, "Hello, Mr. Turkey, How Are You?" and "Who Did Swallow Jonah Down?" with them a million and one times.

Chances are, I won't someday discover a cure for a deadly disease, but I'm planning on always being ready to help someone find a lost dream, missing car keys or grace in the eyes of the Lord.

I may not ever be a wonder on Wall Street, but I want to always be a watchful, caring neighbor on our street, the kind who notices that someone is wandering in their pajamas on their front lawn, locked out.

I may never have a flawless runway figure or a sho case mansion on a street of dreams. But I hope I will always have warm eyes, a ready laugh, an inviting lap and a porch light I can leave burning through the night.

I may never be part of a Fortune 500 company, but I hope, as I grow rich with years and experience, to still be good company.

I may never even come close to being a master gardener, but wherever I am planted, I will always be a gardener for my Master, one who joyfully observes Rule #1: The direction to gently point all living, growing things is always up.

When all is said and done in my life, I don't know whether there will ever be a hospital wing bearing my name or a bronze statue of me in the park for feathered friends to light on and kids to run crazy circles around. It seems there is limited space in this world for erecting monuments.

But I've noticed there is plenty of room for leaving footprints. I'll do that—leave my footprints of faith—especially for the children to follow, so that running in crazy circles is only the way they sometimes play, not the way they always live.

Maybe someday a volunteer biographer (like my writer friend, Carol) will drink lots of coffee, stare at the wall and try to craft 17 solid chapters about my life. I know now that I could be happy with just 17 words—those of a poem I came across recently by Thomas Fessenden. If those who know me best—and the God who loves me most—can someday truthfully say these 17 shining words about me,
I will be forever satisfied.

You built no great cathedrals
That centuries applaud;
But with a grace exquisite
Your life cathedraled God.[5]

Who could ask for anything more? You know, though, now that I ponder it, I think I could be satisfied with just five words. Especially if they were these, the sweetest words of a lifetime: "Well done, child. Welcome home."

Afterword

I don't need to know my ring size, license numbers, the words to the old school fight song or how much pressure I use in my tires....There are only three things worth remembering: your Social Security number, the formula for your hair dye and how many hours you were in labor with your children.

ERMA BOMBECK[1]

Far be it from me to clutter up your brain with lots of useless information just as you close this book. But there *is* something more worth remembering—or worth discovering for the first time—that I'd like to mention.

The God who created you is madly in love with you. He wants you to know Him personally and to discover life as He meant it to be. In fact, He says He *is* life. Maybe you've spent a long time living in your own way, by your own lights, for all your own reasons. You've been there, done that, and deep inside you know something—or Someone—is missing.

The God of all the universe cares intimately about you, your hopes and worries, your joys and hurts, every detail of your life. He just can't keep His mind or His eyes off you. The One who planted the mountains and turns the stars on each night knows and loves you completely, just as you are. He longs for you to be His.

Have you ever come to Jesus and given Him your heart? You can do that with a simple prayer like this:

Jesus, I have lived my life apart from You. I have gone my own way and done wrong. Please forgive me. Come into my heart and life, Jesus. Please make me alive and clean inside with Your love. Thank You that heaven is real and I will go there when I die. It won't be because of any good I've done, but because of Your love for me. Help me live now for what matters and lasts. Amen.

If you've prayed from your heart, you can trust that now you belong to Jesus. Not just for today or for the next few weeks, but forever. "God can live anywhere in the universe," writes Max Lucado, "and He chose your heart."[2] This is such a banner day for you that even the angels know it. The moment you said "Come in" to God and His love, you triggered a celestial celebration. Can you imagine? Heaven is rejoicing over you right now. You just can't do any better than that.

Do something for me, will you? As soon as you can, tell a trusted someone—maybe a family member or friend—about the choice you've made to live for Jesus. (I'm including a few Bible verses to encourage you, too.)[3]

Just think, now you can close this book and open a whole new chapter of living. Sounds awfully simple, you say? Well, God is just like that. Simply wonderful. Simply amazing. You wait...you'll see.

May your roots go down deep into the soil of God's marvelous love; and may you be able to feel and understand...how long, how wide, how deep and how high His love really is...you will never see the end of it.[4]

Endnotes

Chapter 1
1. Honor Books Staff, *God's Little Instruction Book for Women* (Tulsa, Okla.: Honor Books, 1996), n.p.
2. Benjamin Disraeli, source unknown.
3. Dale Turner, "A Meaningful Life: Choose Goal, Give All That's in You," *Seattle Times*, June 8, 1996, n.p.
4. *The Treasure Chest* (New York: Harper and Row, 1965), p. 105.
5. William Carmichael, ed., *The Best Things Ever Said About Parenting* (Wheaton, Ill.: Tyndale House Publishers, 1996), p. 9.
6. Ibid., p. 234.
7. Sarah Ban Breathnach, *Simple Abundance: A Daybook of Comfort and Joy* (New York: Warner Books, 1995), n.p.
8. Tim Hansel, *When I Relax, I Feel Guilty* (Elgin, Ill.: David C. Cook Publishing Co., 1979), p. 59.

Chapter 2
1. Carmichael, *The Best Things Ever Said About Parenting*, p. 234.
2. Eileen Silva Kindig, *Remember the Time...? The Power and Promise of Family Storytelling* (Downers Grove, Ill.: InterVarsity Press, 1997), p. 70.
3. Anne Lamott, *Bird by Bird* (New York: Doubleday, 1995), p. 181.
4. "The Story Goes On," © 1995 Word Music/Edward Grant, Inc. ASCAP/Shepherd's Fold Music BMI (Janice Chaffee/Connie Harrington/Ty Lacy).
5. See Luke 13:4.
6. James Dobson, "Home with a Heart," *Focus on the Family* magazine (March 1997), n.p.

Chapter 3
1. *The Treasure Chest*, p. 179.
2. Breathnach, *Simple Abundance*, n.p.

3. Rosalie Maggio, ed., *The New Beacon Book of Quotations by Women* (Boston: Beacon Press, 1996), p. 639.
4. Breathnach, *Simple Abundance*, n.p.
5. Erma Bombeck, *Forever, Erma* (Kansas City, Mo.: Andrews and McMeel, 1996), p. 194.
6. Maggio, *The New Beacon Book of Quotations by Women*, p. 639.
7. See Matthew 18:1-5.

Chapter 4
1. Lisa King, ed., *Good News for Moms* (Wheaton, Ill.: Crossway Books, 1998), p. 56
2. John Muir, source unknown.
3. *The Treasure Chest*, n.p.
4. Hansel, *When I Relax, I Feel Guilty*, p. 59.
5. Dale Turner, "We Could All Learn Lessons from Apostle's Contentment in Life," *Seattle Times*, May 24, 1997, n.p.
6. Paula D'Arcy, *Where the Wind Begins* (Wheaton, Ill.: Harold Shaw Publishers, 1984), p. 15; see also Genesis 1:31.
7. See Psalm 31:15.

Chapter 5
1. Carmichael, *The Best Things Ever Said About Parenting*, p. 172.
2. *The Treasure Chest*, p. 18
3. See Psalm 46:10.
4. Breathnach, *Simple Abundance*, n.p.
5. Matthew 24:35 (*NKJV*).
6. See Hebrews 13:8.
7. See Psalm 139:13-16.
8. See 2 Corinthians 12:9.
9. See Acts 17:26.
10. See Ephesians 2:10.
11. See Philippians 1:6.
12. See 1 Corinthians 5:1,6; John 11:25.
13. See 1 Corinthians 13:8.
14. See Romans 8:28.
15. Hazel Felleman, ed., *The Best Loved Poems of the American People* (Garden City, N.Y.: Doubleday and Company, 1936), p. 84.
16. Bombeck, *Forever, Erma*, p. 246.

Chapter 6
1. D'Arcy, *Where the Wind Begins*, p. 25.
2. Pam W. Vredevelt, *Empty Arms: Emotional Support for Those Who Have Suffered Miscarriage or Stillbirth* (Portland, Ore.: Multnomah, 1984), p. 114.
3. C. S. Lewis, "The Man Who Created Narnia," *Focus on the Family* magazine, December 1998, n.p.
4. Carmichael, *The Best Things Ever Said About Parenting*, p. 223.
5. Honor Books Staff, *God's Little Instruction Book for Women*, n.p.

Afterword
1. Bombeck, *Forever, Erma,* p. 245.
2. Max Lucado, *A Gentle Thunder* (Dallas, Tex.: Word Publishing, 1995), p. 122.
3. See 1 John 1:9; John 6:47; John 5:24; Titus 3:5-7; Romans 5:1,2 and Romans 8:15.
4. Ephesians 3:17,18 (*TLB*).